Design
DNA

LOGOS

For more excellent books and resources for designers, visit www.howdesign.com.

14 13 12 11 10   5 4 3 2 1

Distributed in Canada by Fraser Direct
100 Armstrong Avenue
Georgetown, Ontario, Canada L7G 5S4
Tel: (905) 877-4411

Library of Congress Cataloging-in-Publication Data

ISBN 13: 978-1-4403-1033-1
ISBN 10: 1-4403-1033-5

Art direction: Tony Seddon
Cover design: Emily Portnoi
Design concept: Emily Portnoi
Design and layout: Fineline Studios

To Adam.

Love you, bro

Design DNA

LOGOS

300+ International Logos Deconstructed

HOW
BOOKS
Cincinnati, Ohio
www.howdesign.com

CONTENTS

WHAT IS A LOGO?

The word "logo" is derived from the Greek *logos*, which means both "word" and "rational thought," so it's a bit of a paradox that the generally accepted meaning of "logo" in English, and in many other languages, is "a pictorial sign," usually referring to a brand. Yet a brand, like most human ideas, is communicated firstly by a name and secondly by images. A logo really functions as a sign or a pictograph, a more-or-less abstract visual mark pointing to a word.

In the early days of modern branding, a trade name would often be written in a distinctive handwriting, like a signature, and this approach is still used today. Such wordmarks required customers to be literate in order to understand them, so a common practice was to augment the written word with a pictograph as a way of increasing market recognition; this also gave products without distinctive names a recognizable character. Simple geometric forms often did the trick.

Whereas a triangle, a circle, and a star on their own are merely icons, when combined with a name they form something greater. An icon is transformed into a logo from the moment it acquires meaning in our minds by association with a brand name and all that brand represents to us. This process of joining symbol to meaning is at the heart of branding. Early logos often resembled little illustrations—literal representations of what the brand offered. Even today, the dividing line between a logo and an illustration can be blurry.

Lord & Taylor, the famous Fifth-Avenue department store in New York, has used some variation of the above logo, resembling a handwritten signature, for more than 150 years.

Pepsi-Cola is another American brand with roots in the nineteenth century, but the logo it uses today (see facing page) has evolved radically from the 1890s version above.

This illustration, from one of the first Ivory Soap ads in the 1870s, serves in some sense as a logo, tying the name of the brand to a visual mnemonic.

Web messaging service Twitter selected a readily available stock illustration by Simon Oxley as its home-page art. Although it is not actually the Twitter logo (anyone else who pays to download it may also use it), the drawing is so closely associated with Twitter in many people's minds that it functions in a very similar way to a logo.

With sufficient marketing support, a symbol such as the Pepsi globe, by Arnell Group, can become familiar enough to function independently of its name.

IBM

Perhaps the ultimate modernist logo: the IBM logo is a highly functional set of initials with an aesthetic styling by Paul Rand that is both beautiful and timeless.

With the arrival of modernism, logos became more simplified and minimalist, sometimes stripped to unadorned initials or a name with no visual element. Such marks still qualify as logos (as opposed to merely names set in type) because they have deliberate typographic styles that are maintained consistently in all visual communication relating to the brand. Ultimately, global marketing campaigns that embed logos in the public consciousness have become so ubiquitous, it is theoretically possible for a symbol to function free of any written word.

In practice, however, few brands can afford the enormous advertising budgets needed to pull this off, so the conventional solution of symbol plus wordmark remains the most common form for a logo, as can be seen throughout this book. Certain truths about the DNA of logo design remain timeless. A logo:

- must have form and color;
- will usually have a typographic element to convey the name;
- will need variations to account for the different contexts in which it will be seen; and
- incorporates visual symbolism or iconography that is both universal and culturally specific.

Designing all of a logo's elements so that the brand is perceived in the way its owner wishes and its strategic goals are met is a matter of carefully selecting the elements of this DNA and finding the most harmonious combination for them. This book has been put together to help logo designers do just that.

In the nineteenth century, iconic illustrations and fancy, but generic type identified brands in advertising and packaging. In the twentieth century, this role was performed by logos and carefully designed elements derived from those logos.

A BRIEF HISTORY

The earliest logos—also called marques, trademarks, or brands—were applied by hand to crates, bales, pitchers, and bottles so that merchants, innkeepers, stagecoach drivers, and dock handlers could tell to whom the contents belonged. In the days before supermarkets and advertising, consumers weren't the audience for the logo—distributors were.

The first trademarks were burned or block-printed onto wood or cloth, or impressed into ceramic or glass using a handmade form. Naturally, these proto-logos were crudely rendered and lacked color.

Mechanical reproduction

By the latter half of the nineteenth century the effects of the Industrial Revolution—growing consumer choice and advances in printing technology—provided the impetus and the means for brands to develop visual identities aimed at the newly created mass markets. Although many brands still lacked a logo, manufacturers realized that words alone were no longer sufficient to address these new consumers. A visual language was needed.

With color lithography, advertising and packaging could include pictures. Mechanical reproduction allowed logos to be presented more crisply and consistently than before. Although they remained monochromatic, logos were now used to communicate brand names directly to consumers.

In the early decades of the twentieth century, the visual language of brands was generally handled either by an advertising agency or by a dedicated art department within a corporation. The basic design of a logo was often sketched by the head of the company, then passed to these "commercial artists" for reproduction in advertisements, packaging, signs, and company stationery. Many logos from this period resemble illustrations rather than the more abstract symbols that came to be favored later.

Early logos were required, by law, to be labeled as such with the words "Trade Mark." This practice continues today with the addition of a small "TM" or "®."

The role of the early commercial artists was limited to mechanical work rather than conceptual development.

By the 1980s, printing technology and pop culture made it feasible for a company like Apple to use a six-color logo on its advertising and stationery.

Popular culture

After WWII, the media-crafted consumer culture in Western countries started to become more savvy about the visual language of brands. The idea gradually took hold that logos should be designed by professional designers. Brand identities became steadily more sophisticated, echoing advertising's goal of stimulating desire for products. Desirability was at first defined by elegance, then by stark modernism, then a streamlined, space-age look, and finally by a sculpted, 3D effect.

Technological and cultural change have been the twin forces driving logo design. From the 1960s to the 1980s, cheaper color printing, advances in graphic reproduction technologies, and the rise of pop culture had a marked impact on logo design, which increasingly tried to stimulate through novelty and excitement.

In the 1990s and 2000s, computers led to profound changes in logo design. Special visual effects such as layers, patterns, depth of field, color gradations, highlights, and drop shadows became easy and quick to produce. As the computer-generated aesthetics of television and the web became prevalent, the 3D-rendered look became widespread.

AEG was not the first company to have a logo, but it was the first to extend the idea of a logo by applying a consistent style to all its corporate activities.

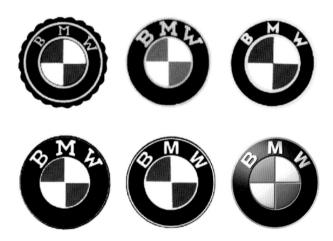

The famous BMW logo, though essentially unchanged, has progressed through numerous updates over the decades—recently by Interbrand—each time better embodying the current graphic technology and expectations of its audience.

DECONSTRUCTING THE LOGO

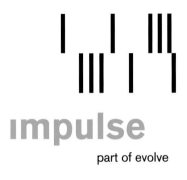

impulse

part of evolve

By the end of the twentieth century, it seemed everything required a logo: not just businesses, but special events, campaigns, nonprofit organizations, schools, religious organizations, clubs, parties, and even individuals. As logo design grew more ubiquitous, the range of obvious solutions became exhausted from overuse, and meaningless abstraction and visual clichés abounded.

Most recently, in a search for originality, the old conventions of logo design have been pushed and broken. The classic rules of the Paul Rand era—simplicity, boldness, and legibility—are often tossed out. Alternative forms of a logo, simultaneously using numerous variations in shape or color, challenge the idea of the logo as a fixed and inflexible mark and replace it with a more fluid visual expression of brand values. The DNA of logo design, as often as not, is now hacked into random little pieces and scattered across the studio floor, waiting for designers to reassemble it in exciting new sequences.

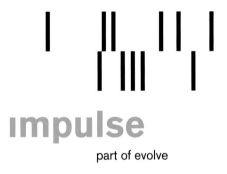

impulse

part of evolve

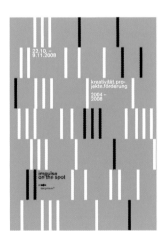

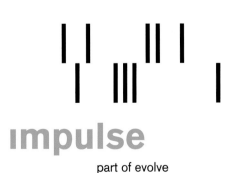

impulse

part of evolve

Alexander Egger is a designer whose work offers a response to some of the intellectual issues in current logo design. For Nofrontiere Design, he created a set of interchangeable logos for impulse, a program by the Austrian foundation aws (Austria Economic Service) in support of the creative industries. The black bars in the design shift about, representing the impulses of creative ideas, flashes of genius, the selectivity of the creative process, and the elements of a musical or graphic composition.

Is a logo necessary?

Some people have questioned whether logos are even still necessary in this age of brand overload, and with the rise of nonvisual media like Twitter. However, most would agree that our media-saturated society is becoming more visually oriented, not less. A good visual expression of a brand, beginning with a logo, seems to be more critical than ever; it helps customers pick out a brand amid increasing visual clutter, reminds them what they love about the brand, and reassures them in their selection of that brand.

In a few special cases, such as the visual identity for the German-Italian translation service shown here, the context of the brand communication makes a logo superfluous, but this is the exception that proves the rule.

The design solution by Alexander Egger for the German–Italian translation services of Puhm shows how the brand idea can be cleverly conveyed in the context of a two-sided letterhead, without any logo at all.

THE DESIGN PROCESS

Great logos don't happen by accident. They come about deliberately, through careful consideration of the values, dreams, promises, and marketing goals of the brands they represent. Designing a logo involves a process, and mastering that process can lead to a more satisfactory experience and better results.

The concept

A logo aims to capture a brand with a clear and simple visual mark. A great logo works on several levels:

- On the most basic level, the logo needs to incorporate, or refer to, the brand's name.
- On the next level, it may impart the offering behind the brand—the product or service—although we'll see why this is seldom actually done.
- On a still higher level, the logo needs to advance the broader strategic goals of the organization to a specific audience.
- Finally, the logo ought to convey an implicit sense of the values, aspirations, and promises the brand lets its consumers embrace.

Let's look at each of these levels more closely. Interestingly, many designers prefer to tackle them in reverse order.

The values

Many brands aspire to lofty promises that are difficult to depict in specific terms. However, they can be alluded to by clever use of design conventions regarding colors, geometric or organic forms, textures, patterns, and so forth that may be universal or culturally specific. To come up with a satisfactory iconic representation of an abstract brand concept, a designer must be well versed in symbolism, iconography, and cultural conventions.

One obvious example is a financial services firm conveying the idea that it is serious and reliable by using deep blue—a color that tends to evoke those values. Shapes and forms can also conjure particular feelings, and if the choice of symbol is counterintuitive, such as a daisy for a construction company, then the logo will take on added interest. In some cases the most exciting solution can be to produce multiple variations of a logo, united by a common design thread, each alluding to an aspect of the brand's activities while held together by a visual element expressing the brand's overarching values.

Interbrand's identity for the Swiss construction firm Implenia uses a logo that is actually a photograph of a flower. This surprising image invites reflection on the company's values.

The strategy

Ultimately, the logo has to achieve the brand's strategic needs: persuading audiences, positioning itself against the competition, moving people to buy. Here, too, the right choice of design elements will have a critical impact. A logo may have several audiences and the same solution may not appeal to them all. Deciding which strategic direction to take in the logo design will depend on judgments about which goals and which audiences have priority.

The offering

People often expect a logo to depict what a company does. In the past this was straightforward because corporations pretty much stuck to doing one thing. Today this is harder. A logo can be a visual metaphor that expresses, in a single stroke, what the client does, although it doesn't have to be. Literal depictions of a company's activities are often impossible, and most brands work on a higher level than merely offering a product or service. Designing a logo that simply shows the product, even when possible, risks making the brand look generic.

The name

When the symbol is chosen, it will be arranged somehow with the name, set or drawn in an appropriate type style or lettering. Whether hand-drawn, or a variation on a standard font, type isn't just ABCs: the specific way the letters are drawn conveys a character and a set of values. There is as much difference between Bauhaus and Bodoni as there is between the Beatles and Beethoven; making the right choice is a matter of being familiar with how different type styles affect perception of the written name.

Logo designs have many more demands placed on them today. Brand experiences are likely to be more complex and nuanced than in the past, so the values the logo needs to espouse must be more subtly expressed. A complete brand identity may include sounds, scents, and tactile elements. The logo no longer simply refers to a brand, but is, in the words of the late brand guru Jörg Zintzmeyer, the projector and the screen on which the brand is shown, and must also be the content of the film that is projected. The logo needs to tell the whole story.

As the concept was refined, variations were digitally superimposed on photos of contexts in which the logo would typically appear, to better judge its visibility and impact.

The logo sets Implenia apart from its competitors in a field where many logos have an undistinguished design.

Once the idea for a daisy in the Implenia logo was agreed, the exact way of showing it was worked out by Interbrand's designers, in pencil sketches. The logo needed to be aesthetically perfect and unmistakably attached to the brand—not a generic or found image of a flower.

The brief

The idea of the brand, the strategic aims, the context the logo will appear in—these are the primary factors affecting a logo design. But do the designer and client always see these factors in the same way? If the designer and client can settle on a written agreement at the outset—a design brief specifying what the logo should accomplish, what it should convey, and what, in general terms, it must or must not include—both sides will have a much clearer set of expectations, benchmarks, and criteria for judging the proposed results throughout the design and approval process.

Peter Phillips, an American design management expert, has researched, written, and lectured extensively on the process of creating a good design brief. His theories and practical advice are followed by companies all over the world. When the design brief is drawn up properly, he argues, the biggest challenge in design is already solved, before the designer's pencil has even been put to paper.

There's no single formula for a successful design brief. It can say "Make the logo cheerful," without specifying how, or it can say "Make the logo orange," and give a reason—orange because it's universally cheerful, or orange because it's the parent firm's official color, or orange because customers already associate that color with the brand. In any case, a clearly written brief gives a designer a set of parameters to work within. In the best cases, the brief also challenges and inspires.

It is important for a designer to be able to articulate to the client the significance of each design element in the proposed solution. Having written objectives for how a logo's DNA will work to represent its brand helps not only in designing the logo, but also in presenting it to the client and other stakeholders when it's done.

Design development

Though practically every graphic designer today works on a computer, many feel a pencil is the best way to begin making words and abstract thoughts turn into symbols, icons, gestures, and letterforms. As ideas gel on paper, novel ways of combining them appear. This is the stage where the first, most obvious ideas for a logo—the design clichés—can be set down and quickly discarded. This is also when imagination comes down to earth, and you sometimes find that an idea that seemed marvelous simply cannot work in two dimensions.

But this should also be the stage at which pleasant surprises happen. Two or more elements may coalesce effortlessly into one, revealing something new; parallels may emerge, delighting and engaging the eye; symbols and letters might begin to play together, evoking the character, inspiration, and wit of the brand. This is the joyful part of the job, when a designer immersed in drawing, focused on pure form, loses touch with the present and becomes one with the ideas floating about.

Sketches of concepts and variations are reviewed throughout the development process by everyone with a stake in the outcome.

Conventions, clichés, and originality

One of the toughest challenges for logo designers and their clients is to come up with something original while remaining within the bounds of convention so that the result is functional and comprehensible. This is the basic paradox of design—relying on a framework of convention in order for the symbology to work, while desiring to push back the bounds of the everyday and invent something new. It can be frustrating, and it does lead to a lot of work being either derivative or nonsensical.

"Give me something like the Nike swoosh," says the client, but of course, there is nothing like the Nike swoosh other than a logo that looks like a copy of the Nike swoosh. Conversely, they say, "Give me something that's totally new," and when they see the result they don't like it because it doesn't relate to anything they have seen before.

Designers use various strategies to avoid such situations. First they familiarize themselves with what has already been done in order to avoid design clichés and steer clear of overused devices. Looking at the many logo books that are published each year, following online design forums and blogs, and joining a design management organization are all ways to gather problem-solving ideas and learn how designers have tackled challenging briefs in the past.

It is also wise to learn as much as possible about the significance of all the elements in a logo design. Being able to answer questions like "What do those curves refer to?", "What sort of character does that lettering style make people think of?", and "What do those colors evoke in other countries?", will allow a designer to use the rules of convention to advantage, rather than feeling constrained by them.

Where possible, the conventions that a client holds dear, or seeks to avoid, should be spelled out in the brief. When the logo sketches are finally on the wall, they will be judged according to the written brief. Do they properly express the brand idea? Do they meet the strategic expectations? Again, the better the brief, the more easily and accurately the designs can be judged.

Presenting to the client

After a designer has generated several dozen ideas for a new logo, the temptation may be to present them all to the client. This is usually a mistake, as clients are often not equipped to make complex design judgments and are unlikely to pick the best solution from among many. It is better to present just one, or at most two or three of the strongest options. If the brief has been answered, it will be clear why the chosen design is the best of all possible designs. When presenting to the client, each design should sit in the middle of a blank page, or in some kind of contextual mock-up on a package, a photograph, or an imaginary ad.

The execution

After settling on a great concept for a logo design, it is time to begin rendering it in a more finished form. Now is the time to move to the computer, either scanning and tracing the pencil sketches, or redrawing them from scratch. Although a paint-style program can be used, most professional designers work with vector drawings, as the resulting files will be far more versatile and useful.

It is vital to get the final execution just right. Execution is important because audiences will subconsciously notice its quality. A poorly drawn, ungraceful, computer-lettered logo will make a brand appear amateurish, compromising its values and implicitly discounting its offering.

Context

Since a logo will be drawn differently for a letterhead than for the side of an airplane, getting the execution right also means considering the context in which the logo is to be seen: the media and technology used to reproduce the logo, its absolute size, and whether the logo will dominate its surroundings or exist as part of something larger, like a sub-brand or an endorsement. It is not uncommon for a logo to have two or more versions: a crisply detailed logo for large formats, and a redrawn version, subtly simplified in minor ways, for use at small sizes.

Logo design has always been sensitive to the context in which it appears, and these contexts are far more complex than they once were. It used to be just a matter of print advertising, packaging, signage, stationery, and perhaps the closing shot in a TV commercial. Now the designer has to consider all these plus web, online video at various resolutions, mobile displays, fabrication in exotic materials, large-scale outdoor ads, and a host of other situations, in some of which the brand's owners will have little control over the exact presentation. Not only are the contexts becoming increasingly digital and capable of special effects, they are also highly transitory.

Perception

Rendering a good logo was once a matter of following a few simple rules: keep it bold, simple, readable, memorable, and make sure it works in black and white. Now, logo designers break these rules all the time. Designs that would once have been rejected as chaotic, illegible, unmanageable, or simply ugly, are applauded by clients and embraced by consumers in a media ecology that demands innovation and places logos in contexts in which they need to do much more than simply remind audiences of a desirable brand image or experience. Consumers now buy the logo as often as they buy the product.

The logo also needs to keep up with the changing expectations of an evermore-sophisticated audience. For example, in the 1990s many automobile logos took on a "bubble" look to mimic the polished chrome relief of the badges on the cars themselves: logos drawn this way appeared more "real" and tactile, the better to suggest the excitement of driving the car. Once customers became used to this effect, and learnt to read such logos in this way, every car company had to do it.

After a final logo design is approved and worked up into all the formats needed for production, many would consider the logo work finished, but in fact it is just beginning. The logo is the starting point of a complete identity. As this develops, new contexts demand further variations in format and a myriad of stakeholders clamor for guidelines on how to use the logo to best effect in their own specific context. The designer's work is never done!

Fine-tuning the final version of the Implenia logo involved painstaking adjustment of the digital images. Interbrand also carefully worked out how the daisy icon would be combined with typographic elements in various contexts. Black-and-white versions were carefully prepared for contexts in which color cannot be used.

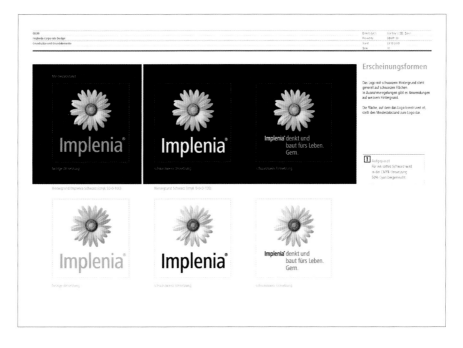

Sensitivity

denkt und baut fürs Leben. Gern.

Imple Dependability

Client	Implenia
Brand story	The largest construction services firm in Switzerland
Studios	Interbrand
Chief creative director	Jörg Zintzmeyer
Design director	Gion-Men Krügel-Hanna
Designers	Clair-Jean Engelman and designers from Interbrand Zurich, Cologne, and Moscow
Typeface	Linotype Frutiger Next Condensed
Colors	Yellow (PMS 1235) and black
Design approach	The aim was to develop an image that reflected the company's values: a careful and sensitive approach to planning and building, concern for environmental issues, and solutions that go beyond the obvious

A logo doesn't function in isolation: it must work with the typography, color palette, and style of a complete brand identity to communicate the values, personality, and promises of the brand in visual terms. But the logo remains at the heart of the system, often called upon to convey the full effect of the brand in the blink of an eye.

GLOBAL VERSUS LOCAL

In the 1980s, Pepsi used a Cyrillic variation of its logo in the USSR, where the brand had an exclusive market. After the Soviet Union collapsed, the local image became a liability in competition with its "Western" competitor, Coca-Cola. Cultural perceptions of logo designs are constantly shifting, often as the result of many hard-to-predict factors.

After an international merger, the Wall's and Algida ice-cream brands adopted a logo with a unified symbol, even though the original brand names are retained in different countries.

In today's global media markets, brands must cross borders with ease. Many designers are challenged by the idea of creating work to appeal to a broad international audience—people with little in common, living in vastly different cultures or subcultures, who nonetheless are all expected to perceive the same values in a logo. How do you achieve this?

A primary focus of concern when a brand "goes global" is the translation of names—making sure they can be pronounced easily by speakers of other languages, that they don't mean something inappropriate, that there isn't already a local firm using the same name, and that the associated URL is available in all countries. Resolving these issues can occupy much time and many resources.

But the visual aspects of a brand identity can be just as difficult. The conventional meanings of basic shapes can change from one country to another. Colors have different connotations. Even font styles can convey different feelings to people in different countries. These are the sorts of issues designers need to keep in mind as they work to "translate" their designs for worldwide use.

Of course, even the most worldly and well-traveled designer can't be expected to know all the different connotations a given design can have in different countries. The globe is an infinitely varied marketplace, and public perceptions are always shifting. A design solution that would have been out of the question in a given country a decade ago could now be considered permissible, and vice versa. Having a local design partner is indispensable for avoiding such pitfalls.

Global brands often find that no single variation of a logo can work in all places, for all applications. Sometimes a different name has to be worked into the design; sometimes a particular shape or color combination belongs to a competitor; sometimes, on the contrary, an old image needs to be retained to maintain the brand equity of an existing brand; and sometimes a brand identity needs to be adjusted to account for different levels of audience sophistication.

In these and other cases there will be good reasons for having global variations of the logo. Depending on the need, a logo can be altered slightly or changed completely. A local logo can be augmented with a global brand icon or tagline as an endorsement, or a global logo can be endorsed by a local partner brand.

Whether the change involves alphabet, shape, color, or some subtle combination of these elements, the same care goes into the craftsmanship of the execution as the original. In the end, the underlying values, ideals, and promises of the brand as expressed by the logo in one market should carry through in all markets, regardless of the strategic reasons that may lead to a local adaptation.

Expectation

Nostalgia

Client	Central Wisconsin State Fair
Brand story	An event featuring livestock displays, merchandise, food, and entertainment
Studio	Erik Borreson Design
Designer	Erik Borreson
Typography	Mickey Rossi/subflux.com
Typeface	Ballpark Wiener
Colors	Deep red (PMS 200) and black
Design approach	The audience for this event is local, so elements that onvey the destination, such as the coloration and style of the barn, are taken for granted. The challenge was to craft a logo that appeals to all age groups—those going to the fair for the first time as well as old-timers who have visited all their lives. This distinguished-looking, illustrative logo can be used in advertising and applied to merchandise. Logos for purely local brands, in this case a piece of classic "Americana," will likely never need to cross borders. As a result, a more literal, even illustrative design approach is possible, without worrying about "translating" the iconography or color schemes for other audiences

THE FUTURE OF LOGO DESIGN

The idea of a logo and the conventions of logo design have evolved over two centuries, but the rules of logo design are still changing. Boundaries are constantly being pushed by young designers and traditional rules (laid down by famous graphic designers of the past, like Paul Rand, and taught in design schools for decades) no longer necessarily apply.

Trends, such as the 3D look, are common—globalization and multiculturalism have led to the popularity of borrowed styles and influences. Sometimes it seems that logo design is driven by a thirst for novelty rather than essential brand values. So where is logo design heading next? Branding has to be sustainable. Its components should be "future-proof" (to borrow a phrase used by Landor Associates). A great logo has to stand aloof from changing fashions and be able to communicate the ideas and values of its brand effectively over the long term. Understanding how the design DNA of the logo functions is the only way to achieve this.

Certain intrinsic elements, like shape and color, are fundamental to every symbol, and most logos will continue to include a name. However, we will see more and more mashups: between technical and organic forms, natural and artificial colors, hand-lettered and mechanical typefaces, retro and futuristic styles. Logos will become more fluid, changing appearance or switching alphabets at the drop of a hat. Such postmodern design is reflective of modern society. Rather than being a symptom of chaos and decay, it should be taken as a sign of vitality, adaptability, and the key to brands' survival.

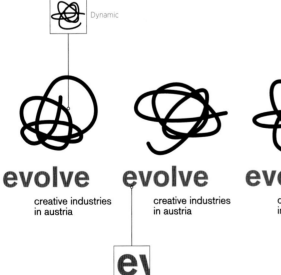

Dynamic

Conservative

Client	Evolve/bmwa
Brand story	An official entity supporting the development of design and creative businesses in Austria
Designer	Alexander Egger for Nofrontiere Design
Typeface	Akzidenz Grotesk
Color	Red (PMS Warm Red)
Design approach	Although at first this logo appears wildly postmodern, with a randomly reconfigured scribble at every iteration, it is reliably traditional in other respects. The arrangement of the icon over the typography, together with the standard Austrian national colors, counters the creative anarchy with a reassuring respectability, communicating that the program's flexibility is grounded in economic stability

As companies place more and more demands on their logos, often requiring them to do the work of complete brand identity programs, it becomes imperative that a logo expresses the brand values and the strategic goals properly.

In boom times a brand identity can afford to be extravagant; companies produce branded promotional materials that are fun, cool, and attention-grabbing. But in lean times companies economize and brand materials get pared back. The fancy stuff seems superfluous. Each part of the brand identity has to work harder, and none harder than the logo. At such times it is important to have a logo that can do the maximum possible to express the brand accurately, passionately, and completely.

It seems reasonable to assume that the twin forces of technology and cultural change will continue to drive logo design. For many new brands, the more unorthodox the logo design, the better. Some logos push the bounds of legibility, which is part of their appeal. Some logos are deliberately bland and minimal, seeking to free themselves from unwanted cultural baggage. In some cases, the once-clear demarcation between a logo and an illustration is becoming confused.

This book gives dozens of examples and case studies explaining how the elements of the logo were chosen and how they work together to communicate the brand. A detailed analysis of these elements will give every logo designer a fuller understanding of the design DNA of the logo.

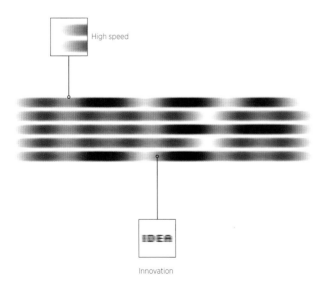

High speed

Innovation

Client	IDEA
Brand story	The Japanese firm ATMJ's showroom of new ATM technology
Studio	Interbrand
Creative director	Hideto Matsuo
Designer	Koichi Fujimura
Typeface	Bespoke, with animated blur
Colors	Black and white
Design approach	The logo, whose letterforms start out as dots reminiscent of bits, or the blips on a cathode ray screen, blurs into a nearly unrecognizable mass signifying the speed of data transfer and offering a metaphor for the ubiquity of ATM technology in our everyday lives

LOGO STUDIES

FOOD & DRINK

A logo for something to eat, or a place to eat it, needs to appeal to us on the most basic level—to portray a tasty-looking item using warm, appetizing colors and inviting forms. Healthy and organic are desirable traits; cold and mechanical are not. Nonetheless, as the following examples show, designers can make use of a wide range of design approaches to denote something yummy.

Modern

Locality of origin, classical

Client	The Olive Family
Brand story	Greek olive oil brand seeking to expand overseas and to sell other olive tree products
Studio	Kanella
Designer	Kanella Arapoglou
Typefaces	Royalscript and Bodoni
Colors	Greens (process colors)
Design approach	The basis of the logo is a stylized sun and farmland, relating to the product's Mediterranean origin. The slightly unorthodox arrangement of the type, together with the symbol, communicates both classical values (the quality of the oil) and a fresh, modern approach. On the top-of-the-line product, organic olive oil, the logo is stamped in gold foil to emphasize its distinctiveness

Client	Vanquish
Brand story	A distributor of premium wines, champagne, and spirits
Studio	Inaria
Creative director	Andrew Thomas
Designers	Andrew Thomas, Naomi Mace, and Andy Bain
Typeface	Bespoke
Colors	Black and gold (API foil: Hazy Gold 4026m)
Design approach	The name suggests mastery and leadership, which is represented by a king's crown. Combining this symbol with the distinctive bubbles in a glass of champagne results in a unique mark that positions this wholesale business brand at the top end of its market, and reinforces both the name and the line of business with a sly, humorous touch

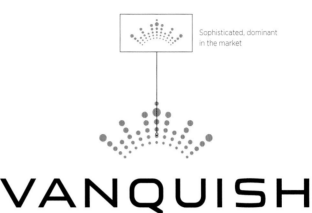

Sophisticated, dominant in the market

VANQUISH

LUXURY DRINKS SPECIALIST

Client	Luisa
Brand story	A family-owned vineyard and wine business in Corona, Italy, founded more than 80 years ago by Francesco Luisa and his sons
Studio	Minale Tattersfield Design Strategy Group
Designers	Marcello Minale, Ian Delaney, and Valeria Murabito
Illustrator	Chris Mitchell
Typeface	Trajan
Colors	Black and white, with metallic colors on some labels
Design approach	Typical of many Italian family-run businesses, the Luisa vineyard is distinguished by the passion, hard work, and exacting standards of the owners. The design team knew that the best way to reflect the brand's personality was to make the family central to the story, giving the identity a friendly endorsement that would attract buyers with a promise of personal integrity. The play on the town name (which means crown), and the use of elegant, somewhat extrovert typography conveys an unmistakable brand character. The richly flowing tail of the L is reminiscent of rolling vineyards and flowing wine

Charming

VITICOLTORI — SIN DAL 1927

LUISA

Generous quality

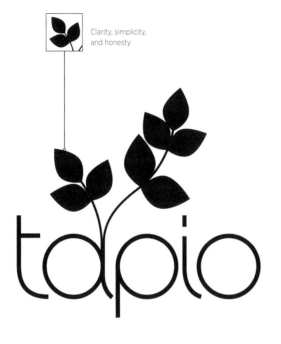

Clarity, simplicity, and honesty

Client	Tapio
Brand story	New, independent producer of premium spirit-based drinks. As a newcomer in a competitive market, albeit with good ideas, it needed to cultivate trust. First launched in Selfridges, a luxury department store, in 2007, the brand has continued to extend its line and grow its fan base
Studio	Transfer Studio
Art directors/ Designers	Valeria Hedman and Falko Grentrup
Typeface	Bespoke
Colors	Red (PMS 186) and burgundy (PMS 1807)
Design approach	The clear label implies product purity and gives instant shelf appeal in crowded retail environments. The abstract leaf pattern implies a natural product, while the color range can be extended indefinitely to signify new products and flavors

Risk-taking

Tribal

Energetic, appeals to both genders

TM

Client	Bad Breed energy drink
Brand story	An alternative energy drink from Innovative Beverage Concepts designed for an active and style-conscious consumer. The drink uses all natural flavors and is derived from complex carbohydrates rather than sugar. It also contains Brazilian guarana and yerba mate extract, along with plenty of electrolytes
Studio	Mary Hutchison Design
Designer	Mary Chin Hutchison
Typeface	Hand-drawn B, based on Hemi Head 426
Colors	Silver (PMS 8001), orange (PMS 159), and black
Design approach	The logo was intended to refer to the name—hence the letter B—and to form a simple icon that could be stamped onto collateral material like stickers, as well as merchandise such as clothing. Most energy drinks on the market have a raw, masculine, sporting feel; this logo, besides evoking the active qualities of the brand, needed to be stylish and sophisticated enough to appeal to both genders

Quirky and contrary to competing brands

Client	Cocoa Deli
Brand story	Kinnerton Confectionery wanted to introduce a fun chocolate for adults that is chic, yet curious
Studio	R Design
Art director	Dave Richmond
Designer	Iain Dobson
Typeface	Bespoke, based on a circle
Color	Deep chocolate (PMS 9180) and vanilla (PMS 497)
Design approach	Since the market for luxury chocolate tends to be serious and straight-laced, an opposing approach was sought. The designer wanted to capture the idea of having fun with chocolate. While the execution had to be clean and precise enough to convey a luxury brand, a playful touch is introduced through the row of circles, which suggest a cartoon of wide-eyed children or open mouths

High quality

Client	Lobkowicz Beer
Brand story	A brewery in the Czech Republic with a 400-year tradition, returned after the end of Communism to the formerly noble Lobkowicz family
Studio	Anderson Creative
Designer	William Anderson
Typeface	Hand-drawn
Colors	Red, gold, brown, and black
Design approach	The brief was to update the existing packaging, developing a more beer-like logo that would have greater appeal at the retail level. To retain the historical connection to the Lobkowicz tradition, a gothic typestyle was selected and the family crest was included. Sheaves of barley give the logo a handcrafted feel, reflecting the brewery's pride in growing and malting its own barley on family land

Traditional

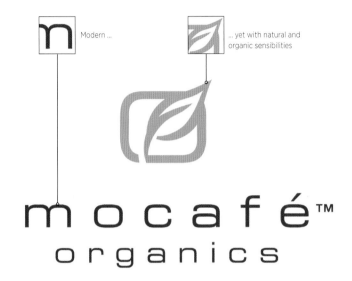

Modern ...

... yet with natural and organic sensibilities

mocafé™
organics

Client	Mocafé Organics
Brand story	A premium line of organic frappé mixes from Innovative Beverage Concepts, to be used by professional coffee-bar baristas
Studio	Mary Hutchison Design
Designer	Mary Chin Hutchison
Typeface	Eurostile Extended Two
Colors	Brown (PMS 4975) and green (PMS 383)
Design approach	The idea of something natural like a leaf emerging from an artificial structure like a pod provided the basic concept for this logo. The result expresses a balance between the organic and the technological. The client wanted a brand that could be visually differentiated from other organic beverages, conveying qualities such as purity, simplicity, and naturalness, while not being "granola" or distressed-looking

Contemporary

Individualistic

Client	Artisan Biscuits
Brand story	Makers of premium biscuits, by hand, in time-honored fashion, using high-quality ingredients. The brand is sold globally, but the products are all made in one bakery in Derbyshire, England
Studio	Irving & Co.
Designer	Julian Roberts
Typographer	Rob Clarke
Typeface	Bespoke, based on Gotham
Color	Brown (PMS 7503)
Design approach	The designers began with the idea of a maker's mark, as used by traditional craftsmen on furniture and other handmade items. "We wanted the typography to be contemporary, simple, and timeless," says Julian Roberts. The modern typeface is arranged in an uncomplicated, yet elegant manner that communicates the artisanal, handcrafted values of the brand, without falling back on clichéd marks or typographic tricks, allowing the logo to be timeless

Client	Duchy Originals (Peter Windett & Associates)
Brand story	Natural and organic premium food products made in the UK
Studio	Irving & Co.
Art director	Peter Windett
Designer	Julian Roberts
Typographer	Rob Clarke
Typeface	Bespoke, inspired by calligraphy
Color	Black (but produced in various colors)
Design approach	The old Duchy Originals mark was considered outdated and too elaborate. The client wanted to retain the traditional elements, such as the shield, crown, and bezants, and asked the designer and typographer to simplify and modernize them. They recrafted the logo and name in a sensitive manner that upholds the qualities and retains the widely recognized royal assets of the original mark, but is more contemporary and versatile

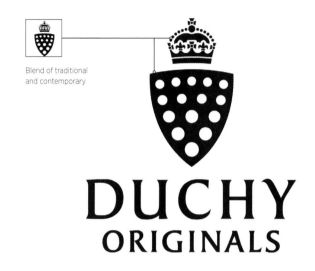

Blend of traditional and contemporary

Client	Fresh Productions
Brand story	Distributes packaged salads and cut vegetables to leading supermarkets around Kuwait
Studio	Paragon Marketing Communications
Art director	Konstantin Assenov
Typefaces	English: Frutiger; Arabic: bespoke, based on Frutiger
Colors	Green (PMS DS 290-1) and orange (PMS DS 36-1)
Design approach	The products are marketed to health-conscious consumers and the client was looking for a style inspired by European and Japanese advertising and packaging. A simple, spare look was called for, since this would not only underscore the brand values of freshness and healthy wholesomeness, but would also enable the packaged goods to stand out from the competition on the supermarket shelves. The designer borrowed the simple shapes and outlines common to modern Western and Japanese packaging, and used bright, contrasting colors to convey an immediate impression of freshness. As an added mnemonic, the central device of leaves and fruit forms a stylized FP

Simple

Fresh

31

Urban, hip, handmade

Client Deek Duke

Brand story A Lebanese restaurant seeking an identity that reflects Lebanese culture and that is urban, eclectic, and youth oriented

Studio Fitch

Art director Steve Burden

Designer Jimmy Kmeid

Typeface Bespoke

Colors Red (PMS 185) and yellow (PMS 1235)

Design approach The shape of the letter D is almost the same in Arabic and Latin script, so making this a key feature of the logo was a natural choice. The simple, blocky typeface makes reference to the eclectic, youthful style of patrons the restaurant hopes to attract

Hand-crafted …

… mixed with modern type

Client O'Asian Kitchen

Brand story An upscale restaurant in Seattle, USA, with contemporary Asian cuisine

Studio Mary Hutchison Design

Designer Mary Chin Hutchison

Typeface Gotham Book

Colors Metallic red (PMS 8883) and silver (PMS 877)

Design approach The mark in the logo was developed as an abstract reference to a bowl with chopsticks, juxtaposing traditional Eastern calligraphy with modern Western letterforms. The rough look of the O also reminds its audience of the shapes and handcrafted nature of dim sum dumplings

Client	Rumors
Brand story	A restaurant and steak house in Kuwait with a vision of appealing to the young and hip
Studio	Paragon Marketing Communications
Art director	Mohammed Alasfahani
Typeface	University Roman DTC
Color	Black
Design approach	The identity for this restaurant needed to be consistent with the name and communicate that this is a place where patrons can talk freely, gossip, and have a good time with friends and family. The typeface was selected for its familiar associations and its well-rounded letter O, which could be used for the interlocking faces to illustrate how rumors go around

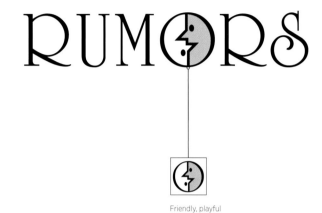

Friendly, playful

Happy, sunny

Client	Okotie's
Brand story	A catering service in Manchester, UK, specializing in African and Caribbean cuisine, with food that is healthy, wholesome, and authentic
Studio	Imagine CGA
Designer	David Caunce
Typeface	Bespoke
Colors	Reds and oranges (process colors based on PMS 145, PMS 120, PMS 137, and PMS 193)
Design approach	The inspiration that would create the strongest associations for the brand is a stylized sun, reminding customers of the food's equatorial provenance. The simple, informal lettering also refers to the relaxed, charming atmosphere of Africa and the Caribbean, and positions the brand with this differentiation in mind

Informal

Delicate

Flamboyant

Client	Fiona Cairns
Brand story	An English maker of handmade, decorated cakes for all occasions
Studio	Irving & Co.
Art director/ Designer	Julian Roberts
Typographer	Peter Horridge
Typefaces	Modern (redrawn) with tagline in Gotham
Colors	Magenta (PMS 190) and pale beige (PMS 7499)
Design approach	The brief was clear: create a logo that evokes celebration, elegance, and Englishness. The personality of Fiona Cairns herself, as well as the penmanship of George Bickham, provided the inspiration for the solution. The delicate artistic swirls are as original and distinctive as the product they represent. Enveloping the composition in a bold circle of syrupy pink gives it a celebratory exuberance that fully captures the feeling of the brand

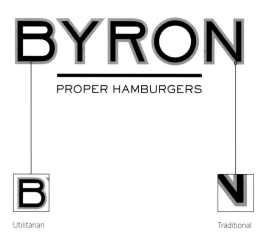

Utilitarian

Traditional

Client	Byron Proper Hamburgers
Brand story	A small chain of premium hamburger restaurants that use ingredients from artisanal producers and suppliers
Studio	Irving & Co.
Art director	Julian Roberts
Designers	Caroline Mee and Milos Covic
Typeface	Bespoke, inspired by 1950s café signs
Colors	Gold (PMS 7530) and black
Design approach	The hamburger restaurant market has a lot of so-called "gourmet" hamburger restaurants—the term is often used loosely and lacks any real significance. Irving came up with both the name and the logo for this start-up client, which aims to be down-to-earth and plainspoken, discarding any pretense about being a "gourmet" brand. The visual solution was inspired by the no-nonsense design of traditional London cafés and butchers. The name Byron and the spare, direct logo support the brand values of honesty, integrity, and the chain's dedication to creating delicious, "proper hamburgers"

Client LaBouchee

Brand story A start-up bakery in Abu Dhabi, specializing in cakes

Studio Natoof Design

Art director Mariam bin Natoof

Typefaces English: Freebooter Script; Arabic: bespoke, borrowing the English L

Colors Brown (PMS 464) and yellow (PMS 130)

Design approach "La Bouchee" is French for "little bite." The designer combined the literal elements of the brand—a bite, a cake, and the name—into a harmonious whole. The resulting image captures the delicate quality that customers seek, and the use of color and shape is invitingly delicious. There aren't as many digital fonts available for Arabic as for English, so once an English script was selected and modified, the designer drew the Arabic lettering by hand, picking up details like flourishes and line weight to make the two match. (Company logos in the Emirates must, by law, include both languages.) The logo is versatile enough to be easily applied to signs, ads, cards, bags, packaging, and the web

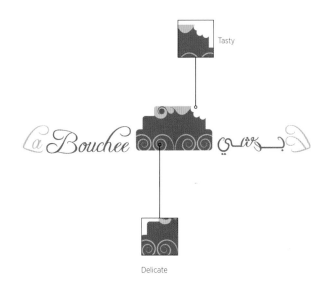

Tasty

Delicate

Client Balaboosta Delicatessen

Brand story A traditional, New York–style deli in Portland, Oregon, USA

Studio Jeff Fisher LogoMotives

Designer Jeff Fisher

Typefaces Serific and Baskerville

Colors Brown (PMS 470), red (PMS 166), and pale yellow (PMS 120, 10%)

Design approach Initially the client, a well-known local chef who already owned two other successful eating establishments in the same city, wanted the logo to include a retro-style image of a waitress. Eventually the logo was simplified to a basic oval design that associated the deli with the identities of the owner's other restaurants, using a design and color scheme inspired by the tile floor in the historic building that was to be the deli's home. The slab-serif font reflects the assertiveness people connect with New York, while the lighter, traditional serif font communicates quality and good taste

Old-fashioned, tasteful

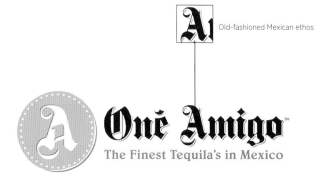

Old-fashioned Mexican ethos

Client	One Amigo
Brand story	An importer of Mexican products to New Zealand needed a logo that reflected Mexico, tequila, and pesos
Studio	Frank & Proper
Designer	Brett King
Typefaces	Bespoke gothic font, with Belwe Medium
Colors	Yellow (PMS 1235) and red (PMS 200)
Design approach	The logo is reminiscent of both a coin and a tequila bottle cap, with the numeral 1 embedded into the letter A to create a unique mark. The visual associations reinforce the name to make this brand as memorable as possible

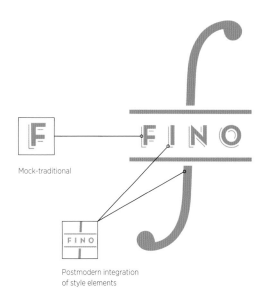

Mock-traditional

Postmodern integration
of style elements

Client	Fino
Brand story	An importer of fine European foods to the USA
Studio	MINE
Designers	Christopher Simmons and Tim Belonax
Typefaces	Bespoke, with Neutra
Color	Blue (PMS 2995)
Design approach	As a new brand, the identity could be developed from scratch. As a business-to-business brand, it needed a polished look. Old European food-packaging logos from the first half of the twentieth century provided the inspiration, and the designers combined classic and modern in a way that is elegant and well integrated, with a very up-to-date shade of light blue

Client	Innovative Beverage Concepts, Inc.
Brand story	The company develops new beverages, mostly for the professional coffee-bar industry
Studio	Mary Hutchison Design
Designer	Mary Chin Hutchison
Typeface	[None]
Color	Red
Design approach	The logo for this behind-the-scenes company simply needed to get across the ideas indicated in the straightforward name: innovation, beverages, and advanced concepts. The two circles at once suggest a number of things associated with beverages—bubbles, rings, cans, and cups—as well as thought bubbles. The minimalist look reflects the no-nonsense approach of the company to new product development, and remains a strong visual icon

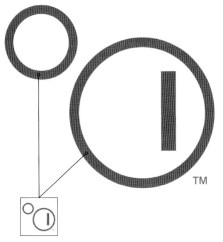

Strong, simple, suggestive of beverages

Client	Quick Chek
Brand story	A family-operated chain of more than 100 convenience stores in New York and New Jersey, founded in 1966 as an extension of the Durling Farms dairy
Studio	Lippincott
Designers	Peter Chun, Aline Kim, and Kevin Hammond
Typeface	Frutiger (redrawn)
Colors	Deep green (PMS 348) and light green (PMS 376)
Design approach	The management of Quick Chek wanted to gain an advantage over competing stores by repositioning the chain's brand as purveyors of "fresh produce," an attribute not typically associated with convenience stores. The initial Q is turned into a circle, symbolizing completeness, and incorporates a dark green leaf to communicate both freshness and quality offerings

Fresh

Convenient

LA BAGUETTE

Flexible formats meet the varied needs of a chain of bakery stores

Brand story   After a change of ownership, this chain of bakery stores in Kuwait sought a complete rebranding to reflect the modernization of the business and the expanded selection of goods for sale

Studio   Paragon Marketing Communications

Art director   Louai Alasfahani

Typefaces   English: Myriad Bold; Arabic: bespoke, based on Myriad Bold

Colors   Blue (PMS 291), orange (PMS 144), and gray (PMS Cool Gray 8)

Design approach   The new owners wanted a fresh identity that would instantly communicate the chain's positive changes. Although La Baguette retained the name that had been in use for more than 20 years, it needed to update its appearance to make it look modern and reflect its new investment in state-of-the-art equipment.

Paragon suggested the slogan "a symbol of quality harvested from nature" to articulate the brand's promise to customers. This led to the choice of a wheat ear, bursting with wholesomeness, enclosed in regular shapes of bright, complementary colors, augmented by the name in sans-serif Arabic and English fonts. The regularity of the image is a key part of its appeal: customers can expect the same level of quality in each of the dozen or more outlets around Kuwait.

In the context of the local market, the resulting identity was simple to apply on signage, packaging, advertising, and delivery trucks to communicate the brand positioning clearly to the local audience. Where needed, the elements of the logo are easily rearranged, for example, a long horizontal version is applied over storefronts where the vertical logo would not have sufficient impact. Secondary graphic elements derived from the logo, like the wavy stripes of blue and orange, are used on such items as shopping bags to extend the identity and allow it to take over the item visually. For more high-end applications, such as packaging for luxury chocolates, a monochromatic white-on-gold version is used.

The logo has two main formats: a vertical version with the icon above the names, and a horizontal version with the names flanking the icon in a long strip. In this case, the bilingual name offers the advantage of symmetry.

Whereas the name dominates the logo on storefront signs, in the vertical format used on packaging and wrapping materials, as well as in advertisements, the icon dominates.

Middle-East contemporary

Consistency

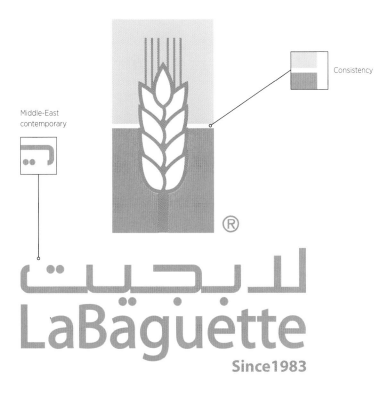

For luxurious packaging purposes, a monochrome version of the logo is printed in reverse on gold-colored paper. The storefront logo is constructed and lit in such a way as to be equally legible by day and by night.

SANTA MARGHERITA GROUP

A logo walks the fine line between icon and illustrative device on a series of wine labels

Brand story A family-owned group of Italian winemakers that needed to update the image of its wines and strengthen its shelf presence in stores, while retaining the recognition factor of previous labels and respecting the design conventions of Italian wine labels

Studio Minale Tattersfield Design Strategy Group

Designers Marcello Minale, Ian Delaney, and Valeria Murabito

Illustrators Chris Mitchell and Andrew Davidson

Typefaces Santa Margherita: bespoke; Torresella: Jupiter; Sassoregale: Mason

Colors Santa Margherita: burgundy (PMS 188); Torresella: gold foils; Sassoregale: gold foils

Design approach Torresella wines are produced from vineyards in the eastern Veneto, a beautiful and largely pristine region in northeastern Italy. The range was not fulfilling its potential, partly because it lacked strong presence on the shelf. As part of a new label, Minale Tattersfield designed a new logo with a vine shaped like a T on a background of stylized flora and fauna typical of the region. The label creates an impression of fresh, modern, approachable wines grown in an untouched environment— harmony with nature. The brand was extended to prosecco (sparkling wine) as well.

Sassoregale wines are made in the Maremma, a sparsely populated part of Tuscany that has retained some of its wildness. The old labels did not convey a sense of the wines' regional origins or what the brand stood for. The new labels carry a fresh identity that includes a wild boar's head, conveying both the provenance and the heritage of the wines. The rest of the label is filled with the owners' family crest, which appeared previously and was therefore recognized by customers. The challenge with the flagship brand was to retain a sense of its long and distinguished history while also making clear its modern approach to winemaking. The designers needed to craft a strong, new brand identity that also reassured consumers by keeping some old elements and following familiar design conventions. The new logo redraws the Marzotto family villa in gold (embossed on most of the labels), emphasizing the family's centuries-old ties to the region, while establishing a stronger shelf presence.

Wine labeling is often a highly creative field, with many wines adopting radical, eye-catching designs. Brands that seek to maintain a traditional image, conforming to classic conventions of label design, nonetheless have to compete for customers' attention against the edgier, flashier designs of less traditional brands. This requires an artful blending of conservative design with modern elements such as gold foil and subtle underprinting.

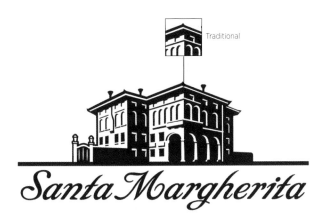

Traditional

The T-shaped vine is detailed enough to function as an illustration, but simple enough to work as an icon in various color combinations.

The logos for all three wines follow the classic arrangement of icon over name. This makes the wines immediately recognizable as part of the vineyards' ranges, as well as making implicit statements about brand values and quality.

FASHION & RETAIL

The fashion business is, by definition, concerned with current design trends, so one might expect the idea of what constitutes a good fashion logo to change from year to year. The examples here demonstrate that it's possible for a fashion brand's personality and visual identity to embrace an up-to-date sensibility and remain relevant by embodying the idea of constant change as one of the brand values.

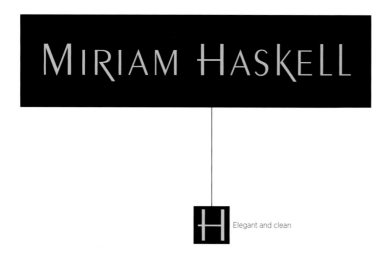

Elegant and clean

Client	Miriam Haskell
Brand story	An early twentieth-century jewelry designer in New York whose line continues to the present
Studio	Think Studio, NYC
Designers	John Clifford and Herb Thornby
Typeface	Peignot (modified)
Colors	Green (PMS 382) and metallic bronze (PMS 8600)
Design approach	The brief was to update the look of this 80-year-old brand while acknowledging its history. The company had been using two different logos: a hard-to-read signature and an all-capital-letters serif font that was visually undistinguished. The designers explored typography of the 1920s, when Miriam opened her first store in Manhattan. The jewelry designs are ornate and complex, and a simple clear look was sought in order to provide contrast. Embellishments, including the lengthened R and K, give the resulting name a bit of personality, while the eye-catching color palette hints at the nature of the product

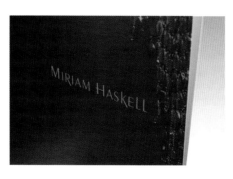

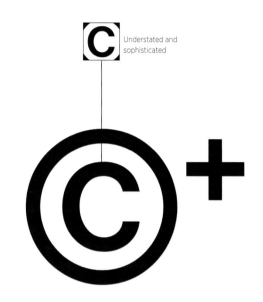

Understated and sophisticated

Client C+ Jewelry

Brand story This jewelry brand takes consumer goods and "remixes" them as jewelry, giving objects new meaning by altering perception

Studio MINE

Designers Christopher Simmons and Tim Belonax

Typeface [None]

Colors Packaging: white foil; stationery: clear and black foils

Design approach The identity echoes the company's philosophy of creating value by shifting perspectives and presenting familiar objects in a new light. The logo repurposes familiar typographic symbols—the plus sign and the copyright sign—to create a mark that conveys the brand concept perfectly. Using a series of clear and metallic foils, the logo is presented in such a way that the audience must turn each piece of paper to catch the light and reveal the text. The result communicates allure and credibility to a sophisticated fashion market

Mystical, exclusive

Client Fair Trade Jewellery Co.

Brand story Canadian artisan jeweler who uses materials with fair-trade certification

Studio Seven25. Design & Typography

Creative director Isabelle Swiderski

Designer Joel Shane

Typeface Egret (modified)

Colors Turquoise (PMS 337) and gray (PMS Cool Gray 10)

Design approach The brand needed to appeal to a luxury-seeking audience, not just consumers focused on ethics. The idea was to represent love in all its forms, using the iconography of mythology and nature. Besides the intrinsic beauty of its tail feathers, the peacock has many allegorical and mythical connotations in a variety of cultures. Using the bird as a stylized symbol contributes a mystical allure to the brand, while conveying the exclusivity of the product through the pared-down beauty of its simple lines, with its curves echoed in the unusual typography

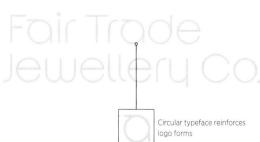

Circular typeface reinforces logo forms

Modern, distinct

Handmade

Feminine

Client	Chocosho
Brand story	Online retail site that showcases young, independent fashion designers
Studio	//Avec
Designer	Camillia BenBassat
Typeface	Hand-drawn, based on Benton
Color	Black
Design approach	Many of the pieces featured in the store are limited edition and/or made by hand. To convey this bespoke quality, the logo was painstakingly hand-drawn and the communication materials were printed by letterpress, rather than offset, to reinforce the idea of the special quality of the goods sold

Client	Gretta Sloane
Brand story	An upscale fashion boutique in Oklahoma City, catering to women aged 25–40, in the middle to upper classes. The store carries many premium brands. The name has no particular meaning, but was chosen arbitrarily by the owners for its associations with luxury and modern femininity
Studio	Mosaic Creative
Designer	Tad Dobbs
Typeface	Bespoke, based loosely on Optima
Colors	Dark brown (PMS 7533) and beige (PMS 4655)
Design approach	The client initially wanted a star worked into the logo, similar to the logo for Macy's department store. The designer felt a classical look was called for, but wanted to avoid it feeling dated, so the typeface was modified by hand to give it nicely defined forms and graceful thicks and thins, implying upscale fashion. Using all lowercase also gave it a modern appeal. The logo needed to be bold enough to work as a storefront sign, while also functioning at smaller sizes on bags and clothing tags

Client	Lankabaari
Brand story	Store and meeting place in Finland, selling thread, wool, and all things knitting-related, that also gives customers a place to sit down, have a coffee and a chat, and knit. The name is Finnish for "thread bar"
Studio	Studio EMMI
Designer	Emmi Salonen
Typeface	Bespoke
Color	Turquoise-green
Design approach	"Very simply, thread," says Ms. Salonen. The client and designer wanted something that would appeal to younger people and get them interested in knitting. It had to be inviting and warm, conveying the idea that the store is more than a place to get the latest knitting gear—that it is also somewhere to meet people and have a good time

Fresh, youthful, and inviting

Client	Velda Lauder
Brand story	Maker of bespoke, high-fashion corsets
Studio	Planet
Designers	Bobbie Haslett and Phil Bradwick
Typeface	Lainie Day
Color	Gold (PMS 876)
Design	The fashion designer had garnered substantial positive coverage in the press, but felt that her identity didn't match the quality of the garments or present a suitably appealing image to her target audience. She had recently released a range of corsets with a vintage theme, so the designers at Planet used the feel of these as a starting point for the new identity. The old logo had a hand-drawn and gothic quality; the new one retains the image of the corset, but is more feminine, with a vintage quality

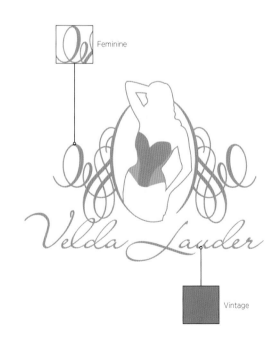

Feminine

Vintage

DESIGNERS
AT DEBENHAMS

D Spare, stylish

Client	Designers at Debenhams
Brand story	An umbrella brand bringing some 30 of the world's leading fashion designers to a mass market at Debenhams department stores in the UK
Studio	R Design
Designer	Dave Richmond
Typeface	Futura Light
Color	Black
Design approach	This very simple logo consists of just type and a single ruled line. It connotes high fashion, without referring specifically to the look or logo of any particular designer. On the other hand it avoids seeming too generic through carefully spaced lettering and well-balanced proportions—above and below the unifying rule—to retain a feeling of exclusivity

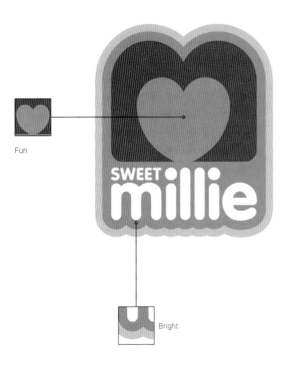

Fun

Bright

Client	Sweet Millie
Brand story	Funky clothes and accessories for girls aged 2 to 8, sold through a leading UK department store
Studio	R Design
Art director	Dave Richmond
Designer	Iain Dobson
Typeface	VAG Rounded
Colors	Pinks (PMS 226, PMS 224, and PMS 217)
Design approach	Although the brand is aimed at parents who make the purchase decision, it also has to appeal to the girls who will wear the items. The heart is a universally attractive shape and the shaded borders surrounding it create a funky, slightly retro M to match the mood of the colors. The rounded, lowercase letters are inviting and accessible

Client	Šimecki
Brand story	Croatian maker and retailer of men's and women's shoes
Studio	Studio International
Designer	Boris Ljubičić
Typeface	Bespoke combination of DeVine and Helvetica
Colors	Red (PMS 180), gold (PMS 465), and gray (PMS Cool Gray 6)
Design approach	In the Croatian language, some letters of the alphabet are modified with an accent mark or hook on top, and this client's name is one such example—the initial S is pronounced similarly to an English sh. The designer took this opportunity to give the wordmark a more engaging character by replacing the hook with a little silhouette of a woman's shoe. On brand collateral materials such as bags and window displays, the stylized silhouette of the shoe is replaced with a series of photos of men's and women's shoes. The range of products and styles is further suggested by the melding of serif and sans-serif typefaces into one S

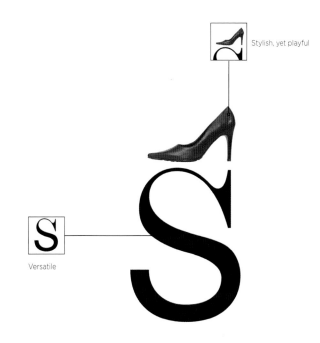

Stylish, yet playful

Versatile

Client	Retreasured
Brand story	A company that makes handbags from old blankets, recycled fabrics, and found fabrics
Studio	Frank & Proper
Designer	Brett King
Typeface	Bespoke
Color	Produced as a stamp, which allows application to tags and labels in a variety of ink colors
Design approach	The company needed a logo that reflected its handmade ethos and philosophy of making things from recycled materials, and that appealed to people interested in environmentally friendly designer handbags. The logo is hand-drawn to resemble embroidered stitching, in a style reminiscent of 1950s lettering. The overall effect is a charming, vintage look that suggests both frugality and whimsy, conveying a clear personality in keeping with the stated brand values

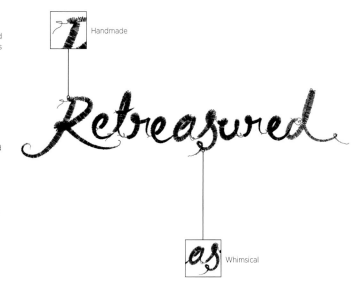

Handmade

Whimsical

MICHELLE FANTACI JEWELRY

Crafting a successful brand mark while flouting traditional logo-design rules

Brand story A jewelry designer based in New York

Studio //Avec

Designer Camillia BenBassat

Typeface [None]

Colors Red and yellow shades, in a watercolor wash

Design approach The watercolor mark combines the client's initials, MF, in a way that also reflects the organic forms that inspire her work. On items such as business cards, brochures, and packaging, the logo is used only partially, giving the impression of being part of a larger continuum. Using a watercolor brushstroke for a logo, rather than a typically clean-edged symbol, conveys feelings of spontaneity and daring that are appropriately alluring.

The concept of the brand—unique works of art that capture the inherent beauty of the materials and enhance the individuality of the wearer—is conveyed by the abstract washes of vivid color, which appear differently on every item that carries the identity. This could not be conveyed by a standard logo with its typical mechanical characteristics.

The impressionistic logo's soft, indistinct edges are not immediately readable. They give the feeling of being spontaneous—almost accidental.

Fragments of the logo are used on business cards, gift cards, and other collateral materials, giving the sense that the brand extends beyond a single object to encompass an entire lifestyle ethos.

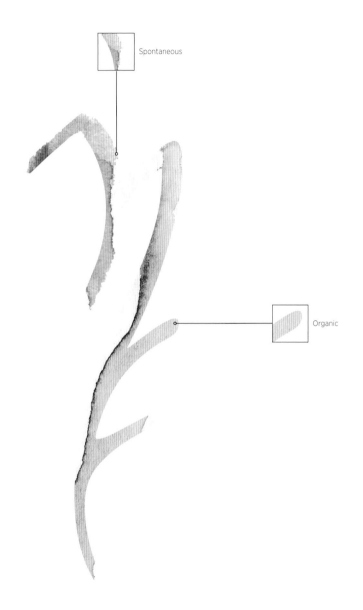

Spontaneous

Organic

The loose, organic watercolor swashes convey
a sense of organic wholesomeness and individuality.
There is a feeling of movement that alludes to
dancing, nature, or even sex. The bright, yet earthy
colors are eye-catching without being garish or
overpowering the beauty of the jewelry itself.

HEALTH & BEAUTY

Logo designs for medical and beauty practices are often a matter of allaying fears and, perhaps more than in other fields, managing expectations. We expect brands in this area to appear clean, clinical, and competent, but also caring and devoted to happy personal outcomes. The color red (the sight of blood) is generally something to steer away from, although, like all rules of logo design, this one too can be broken when appropriate.

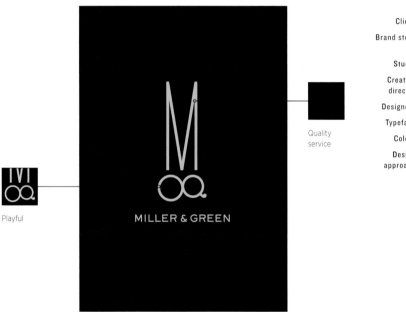

Playful

Quality service

Client	Miller & Green
Brand story	An independent hairdressing salon in Sydney, Australia
Studio	Landor Associates
Creative director	Jason Little
Designers	Pan Yamboonruang and Angela McCarthy
Typeface	AT Sackers
Colors	Green (PMS 382) and deep gray (PMS 412)
Design approach	When this salon opened in 2007, its brand identity helped it communicate what its founder describes as "fantastic hair backed by five-star service," gaining walk-in traffic and breaking customers' allegiance to their old salon. The logo playfully turns the initials into a pair of scissors and, together with the supporting typography and color scheme, conveys an elegant, vivacious brand character that is backed up by the staff's experience, training, and sassy personalities

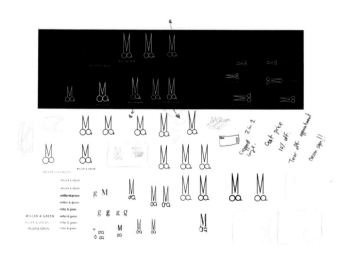

Simple sophistication

Client	Anninos Hairchitecture
Brand story	A hair salon studio opened in Athens, Greece, by Elias Anninos, attracting mainly women aged 20 to 45
Studio	aeraki
Designer	Despina Aeraki
Typeface	Leelawadee
Colors	Light brown (PMS 451) and gray-brown (PMS 553)
Design approach	The client requested a minimalist logo using earthy colors to appeal to his target group of young to middle-aged women. The mark depicts the three main hair types—curly, wavy, and straight—in an iconic, stencil-like style that alludes to the "architecture" part of the name. The type is stacked up in a lowercase sans serif that complements the simplicity of the icon and forms a pedestal, vaguely suggesting the base of a classical Greek column

anninos
hairchitecture

Client	Akadental
Brand story	A modern, hi-tech dental clinic in Istanbul in need of a friendly identity to set them apart from other clinics and help patients overcome their fear of going to the dentist
Studio	Obos Creative
Designer	Ethem Hürsu Öke
Typeface	[None]
Colors	Blue (PMS 632) and green (PMS 570)
Design approach	The client wanted an identity that would reflect the staff experience and the clinic's investment in high-end technology for oral surgery, at the same time staying away from the visual clichés of smiles and toothbrushes. In most cultures, an apple represents healthy lifestyles and good oral hygiene, but the apple image is also overused. The solution was to play on the common shapes of an apple and a tooth to form a unique visual symbol that makes customers smile. The colors are friendly and avoid red because of its painful associations

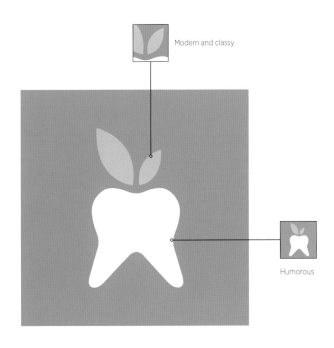

Modern and classy

Humorous

51

Intimate

Caring

Client AID (Accompagnement Individualisé
à Domicile)

Brand story A homecare company in France catering
to aged and handicapped people

Designer Renaud Merle

Typeface Fontin Sans

Colors Pink (PMS 687), green (PMS 7493), and
deep blue (PMS 5405)

**Design
approach** The design needed to appeal to both
health-care professionals and families.
The client asked for a logo that would
show the generous, cheerful, and deep
relationships between company employees
and their patients. The designer wanted
to develop an anagram-type logo, but
knew the design couldn't rely only on
this visual aspect, so he used the yin-yang
idea to show this. The competitors to AID
tend to be large companies with typically
corporate brand identities, so this solution
sets the small company apart with a clean,
humanistic design

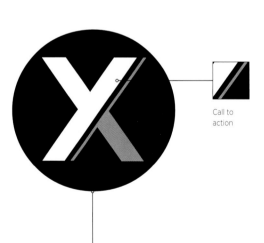

Call to
action

Severity

Client Fragile-X Foundation

Brand story A research foundation focusing on
Fragile-X syndrome, a condition that
results in mild retardation and other
genetic issues including a form of autism

Studio Anderson Creative

Designer William Anderson

Typeface [None]

Colors Black and gray

**Design
approach** The icon of a split letter X in a dark circle
suggests the appearance of a damaged
chromosome under a microscope. Its
highly stylized rendering removes it from
the literal realm to offer a more nuanced
brand message; the organization isn't
a medical research team, but a foundation
devoted to supporting research and
assisting the families of those with the
condition. The stark lines and high contrast
give the logo both mystery (what is this
condition and how can it be alleviated?)
and a sense of urgency

Client	BrightHeart Veterinary Centers
Brand story	A growing national network of clinics for cats and dogs in the USA, providing specialized care from oncology to orthopedics
Studio	Lippincott
Art director	Rodney Abbot
Typeface	FS Albert (redrawn)
Colors	Light blue (PMS 313), light green (PMS 390), and black
Design approach	With more and more Americans treating their dogs and cats like members of the family, they have also come to expect a standard of health care comparable to what humans receive. The brand concept plays up the idea that pets deserve the same compassion and respect as their owners. The name BrightHeart suggests caring humanity; the typographic layout connotes top-level medical professionalism; the ball evokes the playful interaction between owners and healthy, happy pets

Professional

Emotional

Client	Seattle Children's Hospital
Brand story	One of the leading pediatric hospitals in the USA, providing referrals and educational resources for parents and health-care professionals
Agency	Interbrand/Interbrand Health
Art director	Kurt Munger
Designers	Shahin Edalati and Jessica Rosenberger
Typeface	Gotham (modified)
Colors	Blue (PMS 314), orange (PMS 158), and gray (PMS Cool Gray 11)
Design approach	Seattle wanted to overhaul its brand to integrate new research units, attract doctors and researchers, and move up in public perception. Interbrand Health drew up a definition and growth plan for the brand values, positioning, and benefits; and to clarify naming. This gave the design team guidance in reworking the visual identity. The solution is a simple, yet compelling depiction of two whales, inspired by local indigenous art. They symbolize the compassion and trust in many of the hospital's relationships. The circular arrangement symbolizes life and the integration of the organization's activities. The blue and gray remind audiences of the serious medical mission

Nurturing

Childlike appeal

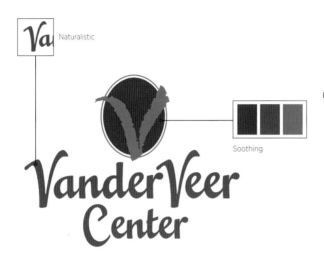

Naturalistic

Soothing

Client	VanderVeer Center
Brand story	A clinic in Portland, Oregon, USA, performing nonsurgical cosmetic procedures
Studio	Jeff Fisher LogoMotives
Designer	Jeff Fisher
Typeface	Mousse Script
Colors	Red (PMS 485) and browns (PMS 471 and 871)
Design approach	After renaming her business, Dr. Elizabeth VanderVeer needed a new logo and visual identity. Initially, she wanted an Asian-themed image, but the designer suggested a more Renaissance style to match the office décor and the idea of the body as canvas. As the project progressed, the colors of the walls in the clinic became the colors used for the identity and website

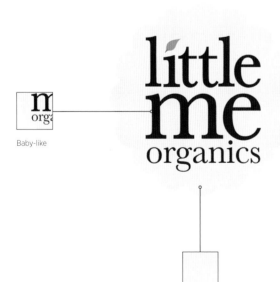

Baby-like

Purity

Client	Little Me Organics
Brand story	A line of organic baby toiletries and skincare products
Studio	R Design
Art director	Dave Richmond
Designer	Charlotte Hayes
Typeface	Baskerville
Colors	Tan (PMS 7506), brown (PMS 490), and green (PMS 377)
Design approach	This range of products, which is made from organic ingredients and eschews synthetic fragrances, was already popular, although its old logo was hard to read and didn't look very "natural." The redesign aimed to stand out more on the shelf and increase the brand's appeal to "modern mums." Since the product is for babies, reassurance was important: the flower icon and gentle typography communicate safety and comfort, but are bold enough to use even in soft, pastel colors

Client	Micheline Arcier Aromathérapie
Brand story	Aromatherapy products and skincare
Studio	R Design
Art director	Dave Richmond
Designer	Charlotte Hayes
Typeface	Optima (modified)
Color	Pastel blue (PMS 2627) and purple (PMS 7457)
Design approach	This brand was established in the 1960s with a royal warrant from the Prince of Wales. In the intervening decades, the original logo had become outdated, so a new logo and brand identity were needed for packaging, clinic signage, the website, and other applications. The designer paid particular attention to retaining the feelings of integrity, authority, and quality that were inherent in the brand. The new logo adds impact and a contemporary look, while reflecting the brand's heritage; it is printed in a vibrant, distinctive color

Holistic

Contemporary

Client	Spa Formula
Brand story	A line of spa gift products for a discount department store
Studio	R Design
Art director	Dave Richmond
Designer	Iain Dobson
Typeface	Helvetica Neue
Color	Deep navy blue (PMS 2766)
Design approach	The brief called for a logo and pack design for a range of bathroom products that needed to appear both indulgent and clinical. The designers took their inspiration from the periodic table of elements, choosing a straightforward sans-serif type that is clean and unadorned. The crispness of the logo execution conveys a sense of purity and high quality, a style that is carried through to the pack design

Pure

Scientific

INTELLIVUE UNPLUGGED

A versatile icon that alludes to the human benefits of technology

Brand story A new line of wireless patient-monitoring systems by Dutch
engineering firm Philips

Studio Juno Studio

Art director/ Jun Li
Designer

Typeface Futura Medium

Colors Blue (Pantone DS 232-5) and orange (Pantone DS 49-1)

Design The logo for this system, which represents a technical breakthrough
approach in medical diagnostic equipment, needed to communicate the human
benefits of modern technology: uninhibited movement, simplicity,
and comfort. A bright color—orange—is used to highlight the
detached wireless cell, which is synonymous with and symbolic of
the product. The warm orange conveys the patient's excitement at
being given mobility and control, and the light blue conveys medical
competence. Overall, the color scheme works well in the contexts in
which it is needed: presentation materials with both light and dark
backgrounds and the off-white monitoring devices themselves.

After experimenting with ideas and sketches
for various concepts, shown above, the client
and designer settled on the version of the logo
shown on the facing page as the best solution
for portraying the benefits of the product line.

The logo has a consistent form, but numerous color variations. In each case the basic concept of a human benefit—liberation by means of technology—is underscored by the contrast between the brightly colored detached circle and the cool color of the rest of the icon.

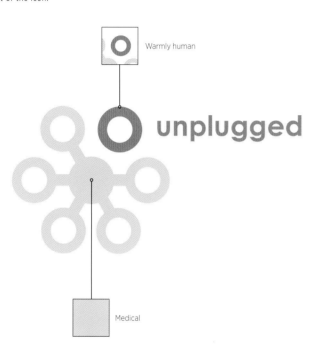

Warmly human

Medical

The color variations allow the logo to be used in a wide variety of contexts, from presentations and product literature to application on the equipment itself.

MANUFACTURING & MARKETING

This is a broad category that covers the makers of everything from solar panels to barbecue grills, as well as the companies that sell those things and install them in your home or business. The key characteristics a manufacturer's logo needs to convey are quality and dependability, reassuring customers that their money is well spent, and that the firm will still be around tomorrow to replace equipment if it breaks. Retailers, likewise, need to persuade customers that their experience will be rewarding.

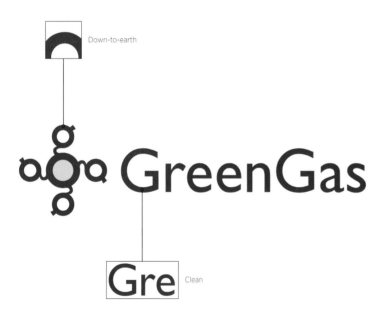

Down-to-earth

Clean

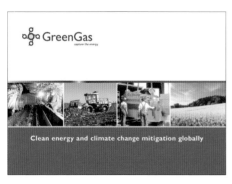

Client	Green Gas
Brand story	A rapidly growing firm that works with coal mine, landfill, and biomass owners to contain greenhouse gases, converting methane into clean energy
Studio	Wibye Advertising & Graphic Design
Designer	Ellen Wibye
Typeface	Gill Sans
Colors	Dark green (PMS 567) and light green (PMS 584)
Design approach	One of the main difficulties with this brief was to strike the right balance between the two very different target audiences: the down-to-earth clients and the more corporate investors and carbon-credit traders who are more accustomed to a sleek corporate style. The brand needed to communicate across a range of cultures including Russian, Chinese, and Latin American. The designer sought to strike a balance between being down-to-earth but not boring, and professional but not glossy; and to have a versatile symbol with longevity and universal appeal. The structural formula of methane is the basis for the logo. For collateral materials the identity was augmented with a motion blur and spots of complementary colors to represent energy sources and the idea of a dynamic, forward-thinking company

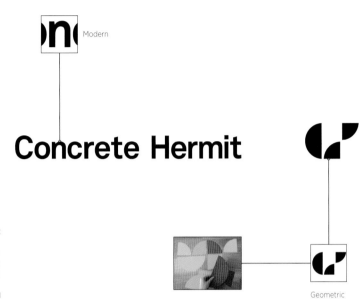

Modern

Geometric

Client	Concrete Hermit
Brand story	A gallery and store in London specializing in graphics and illustration through exhibitions and the sale of books, T-shirts, prints, and other items
Studio	Studio EMMI
Designer	Emmi Salonen
Typeface	Sans serif (not specified)
Colors	Black and primaries
Design approach	The design challenge was to come up with a logo that would not only capture the cool ethos of the place, but also work in different media to represent a store, a gallery, and a publisher with their different needs and contexts. The solution uses simple type and geometric forms in various color combinations to create a feeling that things are happening. The circle segments suggest connections among the different activities and allude to the sense of playful discovery that is at the heart of the brand

Brazilian

Ecologically responsible

Client	Brastilo
Brand story	Irani is one of Brazil's largest industrial companies. For years they sold furniture to US retailers such as Target and Walmart, before deciding to sell directly to consumers under a new brand name
Studio	TippingSprung
Designer	Paul Gardner
Typefaces	TS Gothic Bold and Bauer Bodoni Italic
Color	Deep green (PMS 364)
Design approach	In doing research, TippingSprung learned that the concept of Brazilian furniture was very appealing to consumers looking for well-designed, ecologically responsible furniture. They also identified the need for a new brand name that would clearly suggest the brand's Brazilian origin and emphasis on style. The logo leverages elements of the identity of Brazil itself: the diamond and dot motif is derived from the Brazilian flag; green is one of the national colors and also a reference to the sustainable wood used and the environmental nature of the product. Supporting graphics are adaptations of native patterns from Brazil

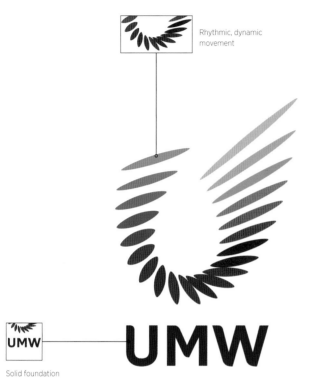

Rhythmic, dynamic movement

Solid foundation

UMW

Client	UMW
Brand story	One of Malaysia's largest conglomerates UMW has, from its beginnings as a car-parts distributor, expanded into other equipment, manufacturing, engineering, and oil and gas. The company sought a new brand identity to help it achieve its next level of growth
Studio	Lippincott
Art director	Vincenzo Perri
Designer	Bogdan Geana
Typeface	Gotham (redrawn)
Colors	Deep blue (PMS 540) and multicolor
Design approach	The company was seeking a new identity to help position itself for another leap in growth. The U symbol refers to its original name (United Motor Works), and also reinforces the unity of purpose among the different operational groups. The bright palette and rhythmic rotation of elements create a sense of forward movement and suggest a vibrant organization that is able to transform and take advantage of opportunities. Meanwhile, the initials have been carefully crafted to make the letterforms harmonious, and their dark, solid color represents the strong foundation of the company's heritage and provides a balance to the shimmering symbol above

Systematic

Productive

Client	Tasman
Brand story	A fertilizer trading company operating all over Ukraine
Studio	Korolivski Mitci
Art director	Dmytro Korol
Designer	Viktoriia Korol
Typeface	[None]
Colors	Light green (PMS 375), light orange (PMS 122), yellow-green (PMS 380), and yellow (PMS 603)
Design approach	Inspired by aerial photographs of fields under cultivation, the logo evokes the rich agriculture of Europe's heartland. Rectangular areas of color are scored by wavy cuts representing the furrows of a plow, which suggest the product benefit— robust fertility. The green T implies the dominant market position of the company— all Ukrainian fields are covered by Tasman

Client	Vale
Brand story	The world's second-largest mining company, based in Brazil, wanted to emphasize its commitment to social and environmental responsibility
Studio	Lippincott
Art director	Connie Birdsall
Designers	Adam Stringer, Daniel Johnston, Brendán Murphy, Carlos Dranger, and Isa Martins
Strategy	James Bell, Hilary Folger, Joanna Khouri, and Sasha Stack
Typeface	Corisande (redrawn)
Colors	Deep blue (PMS 540), yellow (PMS 124), and green (PMS 328)
Design approach	Companhia Vale do Rio Doce had been known by many names and needed a simpler title for clarity and to unify its acquisitions. Lippincott and its Brazilian partner Cauduro Martino developed a new name and brand strategy to humanize the company. The V monogram conveys the natural landscape, a sense of discovery, mining, Brazilian origin (green and yellow are part of the flag), and heart form, implying corporate responsibility

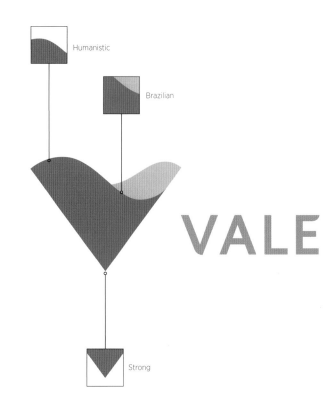

Client	Eurofeed
Brand story	An animal feed company based in Eastern Europe
Studio	Korolivski Mitci
Art director	Viktoriia Korol
Designer	Dmytro Korol
Typeface	Bespoke
Colors	Dark green (PMS 357) and light green (PMS 368)
Design approach	The identity for this Ukrainian maker of animal nutrition emphasizes its use of natural components in its feed products. The bold type is offset by a surprisingly delicate young leaf whose form is echoed in the adjacent letters, indicating that the "green" ingredients improve the quality of the entire product

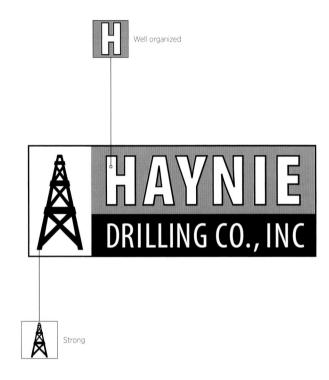

Well organized

Strong

Client	Haynie Drilling Co., Inc.
Brand story	A small Texan firm providing oil-field equipment repair and services
Studio/Designer	Virginia Green
Typeface	Myriad Pro
Colors	Red-orange (PMS 165) and black
Design approach	The client has a deep history in the Texan town where he lives and works. He knew that by giving himself a look of importance, strength, and organization, he could position himself above his competition. To reconstruct his brand, Virginia Green sought a distinctive, timeless, and well-organized mark. She enclosed an illustration of an oil rig, which conveys a feeling of strength, and the company name in a bold rectangle of color. Further materials, such as office stationery, were augmented with a rule dropping from the rig to reinforce the notion of depth, and playful inky fingerprints at the side—the client has a propensity for leaving smudges and thumbprints on everything he touches...

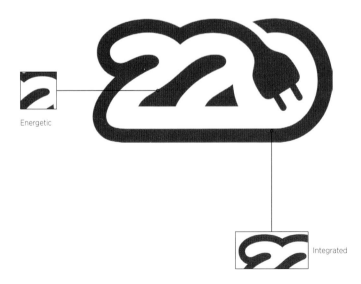

Energetic

Integrated

Client	220
Brand story	A team of professionals providing integrated solutions to electrical installation projects in Greece
Studio	Chris Trivizas	Design
Art director	Chris Trivizas
Designer	Katerina Kotti
Typeface	Bespoke, based on PF BeauSans Pro
Color	Red (PMS 485)
Design approach	The client's aim was to widen its existing customer base and attract new clients from IT firms, engineers, architects, and other enterprises. To do this it needed a bold and memorable visual identity, which it had previously lacked. The name "220" refers to the standard voltage current in Greece (and most parts of Europe). By writing it in one stroke, the logo solution conveys the integrated services and solutions the company provides. The red is intentionally eye-catching and gives a visual jolt to the company's brand materials. Overall, the logo is a succinct and witty reference to the business and makes a statement about their personality and professional confidence

Client	Energy\Company
Brand story	A company that manufactures solar panels and bags to capture solar heat
Studio	Artiva Design
Designers	Daniele De Batté and Davide Sossi
Typeface	Philo (original font)
Color	Black
Design approach	The company's main product, solar panels, is denoted in a straightforward manner using a common typographic symbol—the backslash. This, in turn, inspires a pure, geometrical solution to the firm's visual identity: the values associated with clean, renewable energy sources are connoted by the sans-serif typeface and lack of unnecessary color, while the harmony of the geometric interplay between the slash and its surrounding white space suggests the ecological values of the brand. Repeating the same symbol in the identities for the E\Bag and E\Panel sub-brands reinforces the concept of solar power and renewable resources generally

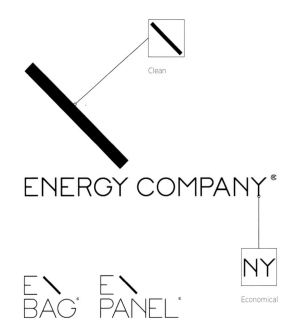

Clean

ENERGY COMPANY®

E\BAG®   E\PANEL®

NY

Economical

Client	Quantum Solar Panels
Brand story	A company that manufactures and sells solar panels for private homes in Ukraine
Studio	Korolivski Mitci
Art director	Viktoriia Korol
Designer	Dmytro Korol
Typeface	[None]
Colors	Pale yellow to orange (PMS 600, PMS 106, PMS 109, and PMS 130)
Design approach	Without any element actually referencing the solar panels themselves, this logo cleverly denotes all their benefits: the warm house, the renewable resource, and the efficient technology. Moving the overlay of concentric circles so that it's slightly off-center with the stacked squares introduces an element of visual tension that keeps the icon interesting and also balances the rigid artificiality with a more naturalistic feel

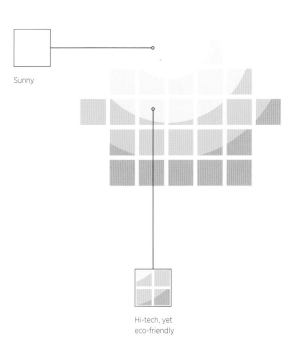

Sunny

Hi-tech, yet eco-friendly

Johnson | Leadership

Johnson Controls

Adaptability

Client	Johnson Controls
Brand story	A decades-old supplier of control systems for cars and trucks
Studio	Lippincott
Art director	Rodney Abbot
Designers	Rodney Abbot, Christian Dierig, and Bogdan Geana
Typeface	Corisande Bold (redrawn)
Colors	Royal blue (PMS 306), French blue (PMS 661), and green (PMS 376)
Design approach	After extensive research, Lippincott spelled out a new brand promise based on the idea of comfortable environments. The new symbol represents vitality and energy; the waves reflect the exchange of ideas between customers and employees, and evoke adaptability. Also, an abstraction of the initials JC, the symbol can be read as the transfer of energy, or wireless transmission. The color transitions convey the flexibility and creativity of a confident leader. The wordmark is a modern, sans-serif type, custom-drawn to give it a contemporary, confident look. The bold weight and stacked alignment add presence and distinction to the name

Modular

Design-oriented

Client	Ton Möbel
Brand story	European designers of component stereo systems
Studio	Artiva Design
Designers	Daniele De Batté and Davide Sossi
Typeface	Bespoke, based on Arial Black
Color	Black
Design approach	This bold, geometric solution uses the extra-bold letterforms to set up a pattern of negative and positive spaces that immediately conveys the company's modernist design sense. Typical of classic Italian design of the 1970s, the modular style positions the company as design-conscious and uncompromising in terms of quality

Client	Power Architecture
Brand story	Computer technology with roots in a partnership between IBM and others
Studio	Lippincott
Art director	Rodney Abbot
Designers	Rodney Abbot, Bogdan Geana, and Jenifer Lehker
Typeface	Corisande (redrawn)
Colors	Gradations of green (process colors)
Design approach	While the brand had a strong following in the industry, public awareness of it was low. Lippincott developed a system to link all the components of the platform as well as the companies using them. The new visual identity promises users the freedom to innovate. The logo includes a "power band" symbol, conveying both the continuity and transformation of the Power Architecture platform and the endless possibilities it offers. A fluid, organic object caught in motion, the symbol suggests energy, flexibility, and agility. The name is set in a clean, sans-serif face that suggests simplicity and directness, while green suggests harmony and fresh thinking

Fluidity

Energy

Client	Gaslamp Computers
Brand story	Affordable computer-repair services in the Gaslamp neighborhood of downtown San Diego, USA
Studio	Frank & Proper
Designer	Colin Decker
Typeface	Semilla (modified)
Color	Light blue (PMS 2995)
Design approach	The firm offers economical repair service to walk-in customers, without trying to up-sell them, and offers straightforward consultations, free of jargon, in a friendly atmosphere. Inspired by the antique gas lamps and Victorian atmosphere of the area, the icon cleverly combines a blue gas flame with a standard power-switch symbol. Combined with an old-fashioned brush-script type (where the flame repeats as the letter l), the logo positions the company as professional, but approachable

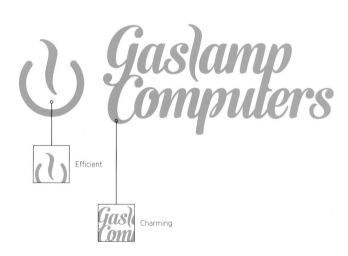

Efficient

Charming

sma | Clean

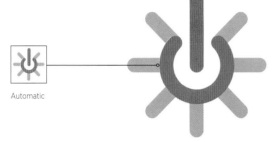

Automatic

Informal

Highly technical

Client Smartmatic

Brand story Engineering company specializing in automated control systems for homes, offices, and technology processes

Studio Korolivski Mitci

Art director Dmytro Korol

Designer Viktoriia Korol

Typeface Myriad Pro Semibold

Colors Orange (PMS 1585) and gray (PMS Cool Gray 8)

Design approach Two universal symbols for energy are cleverly united. The sun is natural and everlasting, and alludes to symbolism for alchemy and modern clean energy; the on/off button is modern and man-made, and as a symbol is found on everything from home appliances to office and factory equipment. Combining the two ideas immediately conveys the field of business, gives a sense of the company's values, and makes a memorable mark that works globally

Client Humanity+

Brand story A technology company dedicated to enhancing the human experience

Studio MINE

Art director/ Designer Christopher Simmons

Typeface Bespoke

Colors Gray (PMS Cool Gray 6) and green (PMS 382)

Design approach The core idea of the brand is to use technology to enhance the experience of being human, so it seemed natural to blend the human and the technical in some way. A personal signature is a uniquely human act, while machines are best at yielding consistently uniform results. Combining these two characteristics into one mark, the focus of the organization is clearly represented in an accessible way. The letterforms were specially crafted to capture some precise human quirks without sacrificing legibility

Client	Calbarrie
Brand story	A firm in England doing specialist electrical testing; it had recently grown substantially due to a merger with a competitor
Studio	The House
Art director	Steven Fuller
Designer/ Typographer	Sam Dyer
Typeface	Eurostile
Colors	Green (PMS 370) and yellow-green (PMS 389)
Design approach	Calbarrie faced both an internal challenge (the need to integrate two companies) and an external challenge (the need to modernize their image and project the idea of providing protection). The solution was a brand identity that would bring the new company together with a consistent look and feel on all their branded materials, from brochures and labels to cars and vans. The angular C could be a roof or a cupped hand, both suggesting protection, while the overall professional image reassures customers of the firm's reliability. The bright palette and atypical contrast help the logo stand out from its competitors

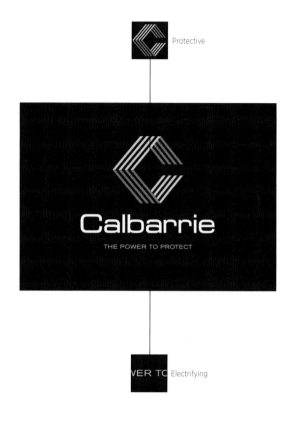

Protective

Electrifying

Client	Asyad
Brand story	Construction firm based in the Middle East
Studio	Fitch
Art director	Steve Burden
Designer	Wael Badawi
Typeface	Bespoke
Color	Yellow (PMS 7406)
Design approach	The agency was briefed to come up with a clean, focused, and self-assured logo to position the client firmly in the construction sector. Rather than a literal representation of the business, such as a crane or building block, the designer opted for an abstract solution that conveys the more basic values expected from a successful construction firm: bold assertiveness; efficiency and competence; and the optimism to overcome technical or bureaucratic hurdles. The bold type and bright yellow make a clear reference to other well-known construction brands, without infringing on them, positioning the brand to compete with confidence in its sector

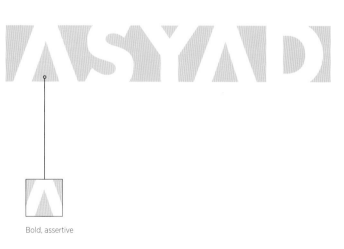

Bold, assertive

Strong

Affordable

Client	Kelly Hoppen Home
Brand story	An interior designer selling through a leading UK department store
Studio	R Design
Art director	Dave Richmond
Designer	Charlotte Hayes
Typeface	Helvetica Neue
Color	Black (PMS Black 4)
Design approach	The identity for this brand had to be bold enough to compete for attention in a busy store environment, without compromising the interior designer's own style, which has a clean and contemporary feel. The customers tend to be young families who like affordable style, so the result is a simple, typographic solution without adornment or decorative elements. The spare, sans-serif lettering conveys all that needs to be said

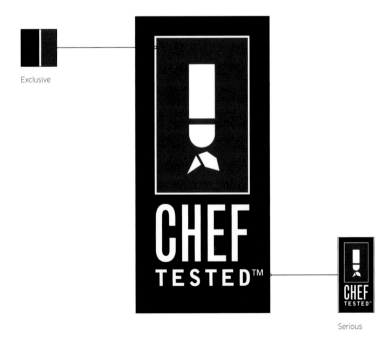

Exclusive

Serious

Client	Chef Tested
Brand story	Barbecue grills and outdoor products for cooking made by an American company called Char-Broil
Designer	Andy Gabbert
Typefaces	Grotesque Extra Condensed and Franklin Gothic Condensed
Colors	Deep purple-brown (PMS 483) and black
Design approach	Most of Chef Tested's competitors featured glamorous shots of food preparation or the outdoor lifestyle on their packaging, together with dry technical specifications. Char-Broil invited famous restaurateurs and tv chefs to give their opinions and feedback during the early stages of product development, and Chef Tested acts as a seal of approval on the resulting line of grills. The logo features prominently on the packaging and signs at the point of purchase and is meant to appeal to customers who consider themselves serious outdoor chefs. Its dimensions (in proportion with the chef's toque) and dark colors contrast with the other material on the packaging and give the brand a high-end look

Client	Das Comptoir
Brand story	A showroom near Vienna for exclusively designed prototypes and handcrafted furniture in limited editions
Designer	Alexander Egger with Julia Juriga-Lamut and Birgit Mayer
Typeface	Bespoke
Colors	Green (PMS 374) and dark brown (PMS Black 4)
Design approach	The repeating rhythm of the jagged, geometrically reductive letterforms connotes both the machine-tooling of an industrial production line and the diligent handiwork of a dedicated craftsman. Like the product, the letterforms are postmodern, combining functional and symbolic design aspects in a novel way, liberated from the discipline of historic movements or any given aesthetic school. The simple wordmark is augmented with a range of graphic patterns used in packaging and other collateral to craft a complex and visually intriguing identity

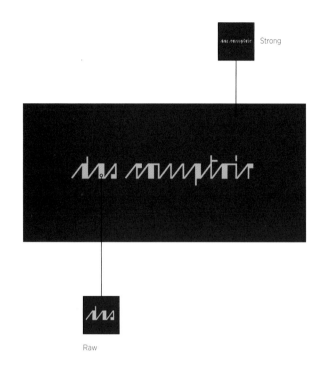

Strong

Raw

Client	Keco
Brand story	A firm that manufactures and sells homecare products for people with disabilities
Studio	Pencil
Designer	Luke Manning
Typeface	Lubalin Graph (modified)
Colors	Emerald green (PMS 348) and bottle green (PMS 7488)
Design approach	The designer went for a clinical look to reinforce the health-care connections of the product line. The block-serif letters are reminiscent of numerous other corporate identities in this field and give the logo a solid, reliable feel that is supported by the calming grass-green color. The space between the letters K and E forms a little icon of a house, which, combined with the Greek cross in the E, underscores the ideas of protection and security

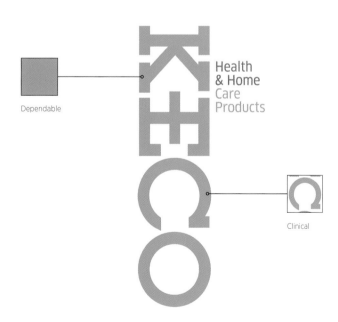

Dependable

Clinical

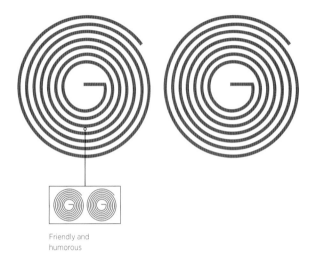

Friendly and
humorous

Client	Graham Gill Carpets
Brand story	A family-run carpet store
Studio	Fivefootsix
Typeface	[None]
Color	Red (PMS 1795)
Design approach	It's not often that a visual pun is so obvious, yet so pleasing. The store's initials, with a little teasing out, just happen to resemble a pair of rolled-up carpets—how could the logo consist of anything else? Instantly memorable, it elicits a favorable response from customers and passersby. As the business is small and family run, the human touch is appropriate, and the identity makes people feel comfortable before they've even entered the store. Using a combination of colors would detract from the strength of the symbol, so a simple royal red does the job. The result is a brand identity that ties everything together and gives a sense of wholeness and harmony to its environment

Humility   Sensibility

Client	Matteria
Brand story	A store selling an assortment of objects for the home, made as sustainably as possible
Studio	Studio EMMI
Designer	Emmi Salonen
Typeface	Slab serif (not specified)
Colors	Black, with variations using various deep tones
Design approach	The store is built on values of ecology (its motto is "good design + smart materials") and naturally, the identity needed to follow this. The typeface selected communicates a sense of responsibility to our environment, and the corollary pattern that surrounds the logo reflects the cycles of nature. By specifying recycled and/or environmentally friendly materials in all brand applications, the identity carries on the promised values of a green lifestyle

Delicate

Feminine

Client	Zilar
Brand story	A start-up business in the Emirates selling silver household and gift items directly to consumers, mostly women
Studio	Natoof Design
Designer	Mariam bin Natoof
Typeface	Harrington (modified)
Colors	Blues (Pantone Goe system 70-5-3 C and 87-1-4 C) and silver foil
Design approach	Zilar's customers tend to be women, aged 15 to 50, who value quality and seek unique silver items ("zilar" is an Old English word for silver). The aim of the identity was to target these discerning female customers and convey a sense of the business as modern, feminine, and elegant. The designer found a delicate typeface that fulfilled these values and modified it to optimize readability, then added decorative curlicues to increase its appeal. The result is an attractive, recognizable mark that can be applied to all branded materials

Familiarity

Friendliness

Client	Pivduima
Brand story	Plumbing supply store in Ukraine
Studio	Korolivski Mitci
Art director	Dmytro Korol
Designer	Viktoriia Korol
Typeface	Bespoke, based on CricketC
Colors	Brown (process-color gradation) and blue-gray (PMS 425)
Design approach	The store sells plumbing and sanitary wares, and thanks to this specialization is able to speak to its customer base (plumbing professionals) in familiar terms. Pivduima means "half inch" in Ukrainian, and the identity takes the common symbol for a half-inch diameter pipe and combines it with an approachable, lowercase italic name to communicate this familiarity and accessibility

71

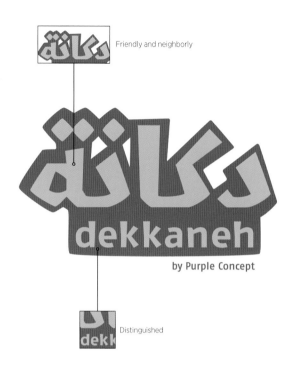

Friendly and neighborly

by Purple Concept

Distinguished

Client	Dekkaneh
Brand story	A chain of convenience stores in Lebanon, catering to all age groups, operated by the holding company Purple Concept
Studio	PenguinCube
Typefaces	English: Fago (modified); Arabic: bespoke, based on Graffiti
Colors	Greens (process colors)
Design approach	The brand concept was to recreate the "store around the corner." "Dekkaneh" means small neighborhood store in Arabic. While each neighborhood is filled with many small stores, Dekkaneh wanted to offer a more distinguished product range and level of service. The solution was inspired by the street art and vernacular signage of Beirut's neighborhoods, especially classic Arabic handlettering and the ubiquitous graffiti. The logo is rendered in a studied manner that sets it apart from the average local store, but avoids positioning Dekkaneh among the international supermarkets. The result retains a sense of intimacy and locality, but suggests a more worldly level of service and selection

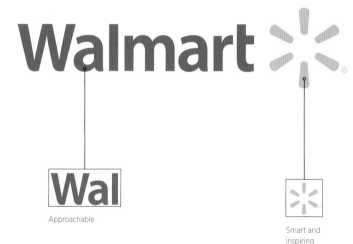

Approachable

Smart and inspiring

Client	Walmart
Brand story	The world's leading big-box retailer, with an emphasis on low prices
Studio	Lippincott
Art director	Su Mathews
Designers	Saki Tanaka, Aline Kim, Jenifer Lehker, Alex de Jánosi, Brendán Murphy, Adam Stringer, Julia McGreevy, Bogdan Geana, Sam Ayling, and Sandra Hill
Typeface	Myriad Pro (redrawn)
Colors	Blue (PMS 285) and yellow-orange (PMS 1235)
Design approach	This far-reaching update came as part of an overall repositioning of the Walmart brand intended to make customers feel "smart" for saving money at Walmart. The new logo dropped the hyphen from the middle of the word and replaced the bold, all-caps typography with a more approachable font. Blue was retained, but a more up-to-date hue was selected, and yellow was introduced as a secondary color. A new "spark" symbol to the right of the name replaced the five-pointed star from the middle. The spark connotes the energy of "living better." The top of the spark was designed to be the W and the bottom of the spark the m of the name

Elegant

Bold

Client	ABA (Ali Bin Ali)
Brand story	A conglomerate encompassing sales and distribution, retail, and other services such as travel, medical, publishing, and technology
Studio	Fitch
Art director	Steve Burden
Designer	Marieline Halabi
Typeface	Bespoke
Color	Blue (PMS 2935)
Design approach	The extensive and varied activities of this large, traditional Middle Eastern company made coming up with an all-encompassing symbol a challenge. The firm's heritage was a strength, but it also needed to project a contemporary image. The new mark mixes classicism with boldness and clarity, simplifying the identity in order to communicate in a more resonant way in the marketplace. It retains a sense of heritage while being forward-looking and easy to read

Classy

Exclusive

Client	360° Mall
Brand story	A shopping mall in Kuwait aspiring to the high-end consumer
Studio	Fitch
Art director	Anis Bengiuma
Designers	Hammad Iqbal and Nuno Pereira
Typeface	Bespoke
Colors	Orange (PMS 1655) and black
Design approach	The new mall, operated by Tamdeen, seeks to present the world's best brands in a prestigious setting. A set of numerals was custom-designed to reflect this exclusivity in an identity that can act as an umbrella over other premium brands. The contrasting thick-and-thin strokes hark back to classy images of art deco, while the stark black forms and the generous white spaces they define give an impression of sophistication. The little orange dot adds a touch of luxury and alludes to the desert sun, calling to mind centuries of Arab trade that brought together sought-after goods from East and West

SCHINDLER

Updating a well-known logo to bring its expression of brand values into the twenty-first century

Brand story   Global manufacturer of escalators, elevators, and moving walkways

Studio   Interbrand

Art directors   Andreas Rotzler and Jürgen Kaske

Designers   Gernot Honsel, Martina Gees, Christoph Stadler, Janina Berger, and Dennis Oswald

Typeface   Frutiger Next Bold (hand adjusted)

Colors   Metallic silver, black, and red (PMS 485)

Design approach   To help reposition Schindler as a leader among several otherwise similar manufacturers of elevators and moving walkways, Interbrand proposed redefining the brand in terms of urban mobility. The previous logo, based on a classic design going back a century, presented several practical and aesthetic drawbacks, looked outdated, and, with its vertical elements, was awkward to use in some contexts. Nevertheless the germ of the logo, a triangle within a circle, still had many merits, not least its wide recognition among the public. The solution is fairly close to the original, but updated in the following important ways:

- The logo was given dimension. Raising the triangle, which signifies an aspiration to be at the peak, from the surrounding disc creates a sense of dynamism and motion.
- The circle was retained to embody tradition and remind audiences of the common point of contact between human and machine—the elevator button.
- The whole was rendered in a futuristic chrome styling, in keeping with the gleaming materials used in most of Schindler's products.
- The name was recast in a new typeface, in bright red. Still sans serif like the old version, it has thick-and-thin nuances recalling the firm's classic heritage, which the old version was missing.
- The long vertical bars that had been part of the previous logo were removed and adapted into a secondary, less frequently used graphic element.

As part of a complex identity redesign, the new logo helps position the brand visually to move forward (and upward) into the future.

The redesigned logo needed to maintain the broad recognition enjoyed by the old version as a result of its wide visibility in buildings throughout the world. The trick was to hold onto some key aspects of the logo, while changing others to achieve the needed improvement.

Although the old form of the logo had merits, the design team detected numerous opportunities for improving on its visibility by carefully recrafting and modernizing it to better reflect the brand's contemporary values.

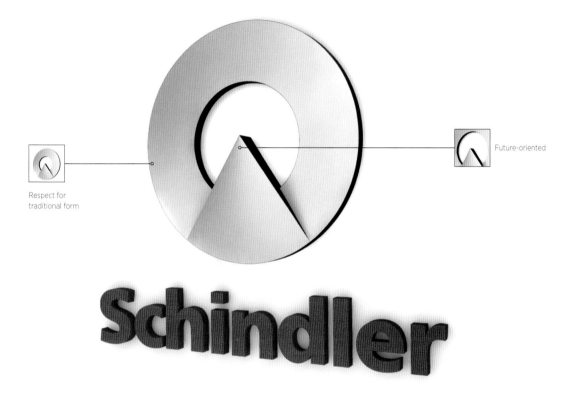

Respect for
traditional form

Future-oriented

After agreeing on the fundamental concept,
the designers' next step was to make quick pencil
sketches to determine the ideal basic form in 3D.

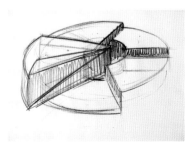
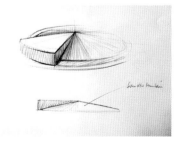
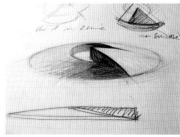

Once the basic shape had been determined, precisely detailed digital files were created as a basis for rendering the logo in different versions to suit the many contexts in which it would appear; not just in print and on screen, but fabricated in 3D for application to equipment, signs, and other contexts.

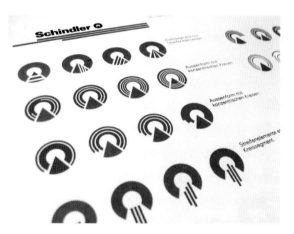

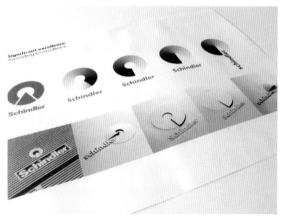

Variations were developed to show the logo in the many different contexts in which it is needed: flat and 3D, color and monochrome, printed and lit.

ARTOIL

Making a new logo work on several levels at a gas station forecourt

Brand story A chain of gas stations in the Russian Federation

Studio Minale Tattersfield Design Strategy Group

Art director David Davis

Designers Igor Astrologo and Peter Brown

Typeface Etelka

Colors Orange (PMS Orange 021), blue (PMS Blue 072), and magenta (PMS 204), complemented by light green (PMS 382), yellow (PMS 129), and pink (PMS 220)

Design approach The idea behind Artoil was to create a distinctive and friendly brand that would stand apart from the more established Russian oil companies and challenge their more traditional-looking brands. The design team sought to create a logo that would express the company's novel customer-centered approach to retail, without becoming too playful, and maintain a strong corporate identity in the process.
The logo design was driven by the brand promise of being "better together." It shows the merging of the primary (fuel, food, and auto service) and secondary retail offerings, centered around the customer, who is at the heart of things. The shapes manage to balance the precision of science and technology with the colorfulness and playful approach of retail and leisure. The vibrant color palette and rounded forms help the brand achieve a high level of visibility in the otherwise dull and rigid Russian landscape.

One of the principal challenges in designing for a gas station is that the logo has to "read" well at a distance as well as close up, by day as well as by night, in outdoor as well as indoor spaces. This requires both good design and careful planning of the sign fabrication.

Like most logos, there are two components: a symbol and a wordmark. Their interaction in various contexts must be carefully thought out.

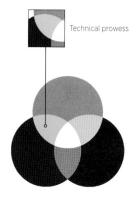

Technical prowess

Elements of the logo, such as color and typography, can be adopted for secondary elements of the brand's graphic identity, for example on signs.

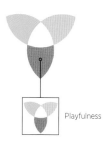

Playfulness

"Better Together"

The logo is a culmination of a conceptual development that begins with fundamental brand values and explores ways of making those abstract ideas visually tangible.

ACHERER

A simple, conceptual design that affords dozens of variations

Brand story Retail store selling flowers, sweets, and pastries in the historic center of Bruneck, Italy

Designer Alexander Egger

Typeface Mrs Eaves

Colors Light green (PMS 396), orange (PMS 109), mauve (PMS 257), and pink (PMS 226)

Design approach This store in the northern Italian town of Bruneck, a traditionally German-speaking area, is actually two stores joined by a large passageway. The logo shows two circles united to form an abstract letter A—the initial of the owner. This clean, modern-looking, and geometrical icon stands for precision and the modern aesthetic of the store's interior, and conveys the trendiness of its products. At the same time it is combined with a wordmark set in a traditional serif font, reflecting the classical tradition and craftsmanship of the high-class florist and chocolatier, as well as the historical setting of the store.

The contrast between the old and new is further reflected in another contrasting pair: white combined with a bright color. The clean white surface provides a neutral backdrop to the products, highlighted by a brightly colored backing. A white front is always backed by a bright color, whether in stationery, packaging, or shopping bags, whose bright insides produce a surprise effect (like biting into a filled chocolate). For the store's opening, a palette of four colors, which could be changed with each subsequent season, was selected. The website is a dynamic presentation. The navigation consists of movable color bars with the main menu items. With each click, the background image changes to show another aspect of the store and its products. The client updates the images through a simple content-management system, keeping the identity fresh and current.

The understated, modern look of the logo is matched by its scale and discreet placement in the modern interior of the store, as well as the tags on the desserts and floral arrangements. The whole design speaks of exquisite quality and exclusive taste.

ACH High-class

In addition to its use within the store, the logo is applied in modest proportions to the website, where the background images and arrangement of links are constantly changing.

REAL ESTATE & DEVELOPMENT

By nature a conservative category, given the large and more or less permanent nature of the transactions involved, real estate nevertheless can offer designers the chance to take a liberal, unconventional approach. As in other fields, firms seek to stand out and project an upbeat personality, while still conveying basic brand qualities such as security and a desirable location.

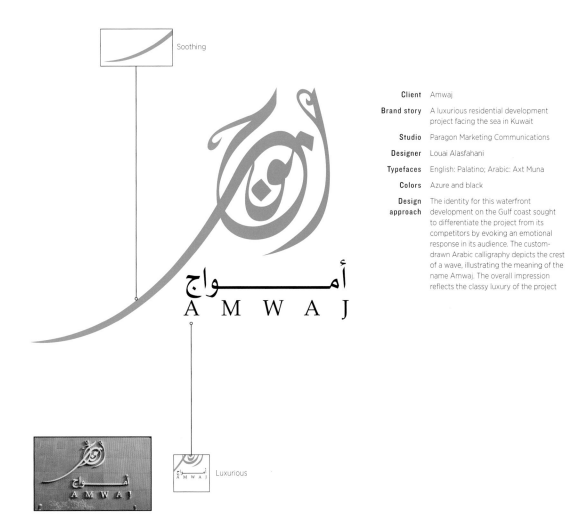

Soothing

Luxurious

Client	Amwaj
Brand story	A luxurious residential development project facing the sea in Kuwait
Studio	Paragon Marketing Communications
Designer	Louai Alasfahani
Typefaces	English: Palatino; Arabic: Axt Muna
Colors	Azure and black
Design approach	The identity for this waterfront development on the Gulf coast sought to differentiate the project from its competitors by evoking an emotional response in its audience. The custom-drawn Arabic calligraphy depicts the crest of a wave, illustrating the meaning of the name Amwaj. The overall impression reflects the classy luxury of the project

Client	Ginger Nobles & Susan Baldwin
Brand story	A pair of American real-estate agents who cater to an upper-class residential market, selling multimillion-dollar homes
Studio	Mosaic Creative
Designer	Tad Dobbs
Typefaces	Filosofia Unicase and Scala
Colors	Bronze (PMS 462) and blue (PMS 5425)
Design approach	The women, whom the designer Tad Dobbs describes as "bubbly and fun," needed a business logo that would convey their teamwork and personalities and speak to their upper-class clients. "I looked toward classic type like Bodoni and Garamond, with nice thicks and thins," he says. The mark, combining the g and s of Ginger and Susan, shows their teamwork, and is a nod to the monogrammed towels often placed in the bathrooms of fancy homes. The use of a thick-and-thin typeface, together with the mixing of capitals and lowercase, gives the mark a premium feel and keeps the women's personalities foremost in mind

Classic

Elegant

Client	Dock
Brand story	An ecologically sensitive, mixed-use development in a former dockland area along the River Vltava in east Prague
Studio	Creative Zone Lavmi
Designer	Babeta Ondrová
Typeface	DIN
Color	Blue (PMS 284)
Design approach	The project, occupying a backwater on a bend in the river adjacent to a public park, was based on the idea of minimizing the ecological impact of new development. It uses architecture and design to make the most of existing resources and allow people to live, work, and relax in harmony with their surroundings. The logo reflects this philosophy: bold, sans-serif lettering conveys the unpretentious architectural solutions, and the merging of the O and C reinforce the idea of using available resources effectively, while also alluding to the meandering of the river

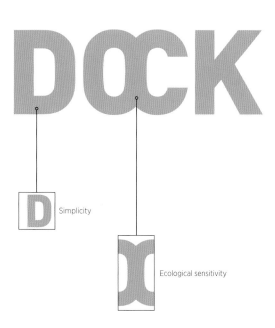

Simplicity

Ecological sensitivity

Organization

Professionalism

Client	Housale Property Development
Brand story	A new firm based on the Greek island of Corfu, serving locals and foreigners who wish to acquire property there
Studio	Chris Trivizas | Design
Art director	Chris Trivizas
Designer	Katerina Kotti
Typeface	PF BeauSans Pro
Colors	Yellow (PMS 123) and black (PMS Black 2)
Design approach	The name, which combines the English words "house" and "sale," indicates what the company does, and the logo design conveys something about how they do it. The well-balanced proportions give an immediate feeling of competence; the house icon within the circle points to organization and diligence while the yellow and dark gray color combination suggests construction signs and reinforces the idea that the company is dependable. A little visual play in the icon—a ladder that is also a letter H—puts customers at ease without compromising the sense of professionalism

Supportive

Upbeat

Client	Settlement Housing Fund, Inc.
Brand story	Builds and maintains affordable housing for low- and moderate-income families
Studio	Designation
Art directors	David Sellery and Carol Lamberg
Designer	Mike Quon
Typeface	Franklin Gothic Condensed
Colors	Yellow (PMS 142), blue (PMS 3005), and green (PMS 376)
Design approach	This nonprofit, affordable-housing developer needed to update its image and increase its appeal to corporate partners and philanthropic funding. It needed a bold, optimistic identity that would reflect its urban operations and communicate its positive impact on the lives of those it serves by providing quality, affordable housing and harmonious communities

Client	Paladin Group
Brand story	A property management firm providing property services in the UK through a portfolio of residential and commercial businesses
Studio	The House
Art director	Steven Fuller
Designer/ Typographer	Sam Dyer
Typeface	Trajan
Color	Red (PMS 484)
Design approach	"Paladin" means "protector," of people and of property. Simply enlarging the letter A and removing its crossbar conveys stature and security, and communicates the idea of protection simply and effectively. The new identity allows employees to articulate the company values with greater clarity, giving them an increased sense of pride

PAL A DIN

P Competence

Λ Protectiveness

Client	Gala Realty
Brand story	A realty agency in Ukraine
Studio	Korolivski Mitci
Art director	Viktoriia Korol
Designer	Dmytro Korol
Typeface	Bespoke
Color	Orange (PMS 130)
Design approach	This style of logo, with letterforms distorted to form a simple picture, was popular during the middle of the twentieth century, though it has now fallen out of fashion in many countries. Nonetheless, this example shows that, when well executed, it can communicate clearly, impart character, and even add a touch of humor to a brand. The heavyset letterforms show dependability and seriousness, while the bright orange saves them from becoming too oppressive

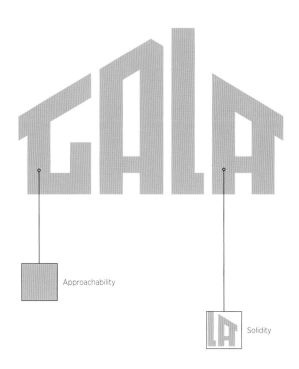

Approachability

Solidity

Natural

Light, integrated

بوابة الشمال
North Gate

Client	North Gate (Equinox)
Brand story	A mixed-use development near Doha in Qatar, with natural greenery amid the retail, living, and working spaces
Studio	Fitch
Art director	Anis Bengiuma
Designer	Shaghig Anserlian
Typeface	Bespoke
Color	Green (PMS 3145)
Design approach	The icon combines a representation of the wind with an abstract compass that shows the wind direction. The swirling mark and light, elegant typeface is grounded in North Gate's location on the Gulf coast, and presents the development as a world-class experience with a high level of design and relaxing comfort

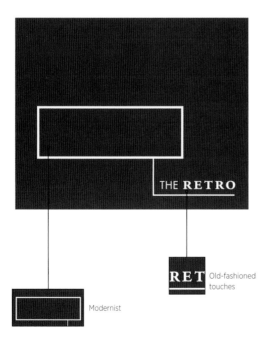

Modernist

THE RETRO

Old-fashioned touches

Client	The Retro
Brand story	A condominium building in New York City that began as two buildings—an old one (The Retro) and a new one (The Modern)—that merged and needed a joint identity. Due to economic hard times, The Modern was shelved, and only The Retro came to life
Studio	Think Studio, NYC
Designers	John Clifford and Herb Thornby
Copywriter	Mary-Catherine Jones
Typefaces	Adobe Garamond and Futura
Color	Red (process color)
Design approach	To contain costs, the marketing for the two building projects was to be done in tandem, with a common visual theme for the two buildings. The designer came up with a rectangle for each—horizontal for The Retro and vertical for The Modern—and complementary styles for the typography and color palettes. Using a visual icon for the building, rather than just a typographic treatment of the address, helps make it more memorable, and this is reinforced with a series of color boxes for other branding applications

Client	King-Dome
Brand story	An Italian house-building firm whose brand position is "regal houses"
Studio	Artiva Design
Designers	Daniele De Batté and Davide Sossi
Typeface	Helvetica
Color	Gold (PMS 8003)
Design approach	The very simple repetition of the lines of the initial letter project confidence and a sense of quality. By emphasizing the angles of the letterform, the logo suggests a shield or the stripes of a regal coat of arms, in minimalist style, as well as the designed spaces of houses

Client	Better Homes – Libya
Brand story	A company that sells and rents homes, mostly in locations near the sea in Libya, an emerging real-estate market
Studio	Paragon Marketing Communications
Designer	Konstantin Assenov
Typeface	Alter Times Bold
Colors	Blues (process colors)
Design approach	The proximity of the homes to the sea provided the initial idea for a symbol that combines Mediterranean colors with the bright white stucco typical of North African architecture. The letters b and h are incorporated with a little house, making the client's business perfectly clear. The overall impression is homely—the properties are marketed for personal enjoyment, rather than investment—but at the same time serious, with a corporate air

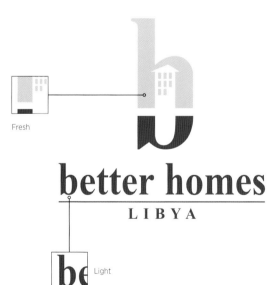

THE PORT OF LONG BEACH

Using logo design to fulfill a brand's broader strategic goals, with an appeal beyond the immediate customer base

Client	The Port of Long Beach
Brand story	A major shipping port in southern California needed a fresh brand identity to help convince nearby communities that it would be a good neighbor and not a threat
Studio	Siegel+Gale
Creative director	Sven Seger
Design director	Marcus Bartlett
Senior designer	Monica Chai
Typeface	Fedra Sans
Colors	Multicolored blend

Design approach After many years of steady growth, the port facility began to meet resistance to its plans for further expansion from neighboring communities who feared it would threaten the natural environment and their way of life. To help find common ground between the goals of healthy economic growth and sensitivity to community concerns, Siegel+Gale recommended that the Port of Long Beach reinvent its brand in more emotional terms, emphasizing harmony, healthy living, and a balance between thriving trade and a thriving local community. It quickly became clear that this would be best achieved through a new brand concept of "shaping a vibrant community."

The Port of Long Beach didn't need to sell itself to shipping customers—its business was going just fine—it needed to position itself as a catalyst for advancing economic and social interests, and as a passionate defender of their values: protecting the ecosystem, living and working in harmony, and building a flourishing community.

The logo integrates all the elements of the community—a ship, people, buildings, trees, seabirds, fish—into a single flourishing world, painted in vibrant colors that move like a watercolor, capturing the local spirit. The final logo implies change, progressive thinking, and growth. It has an organic, youthful optimism that is typically Californian.

The logo is visually striking and bold enough to work in a variety of contexts—even in monochrome.

A complex, meticulously crafted icon represents the many facets of port life beyond shipping. The right proportions ensure clarity and readability.

Harmonious

The Port of
LONG BEACH

Your Environmentally Friendly Port

Reassuring, optimistic

The process of developing the mark for this logo involved carefully selecting and sizing its individual elements and blending them into a harmonious whole. The final version also incorporates a subtly abstract outline of the United States.

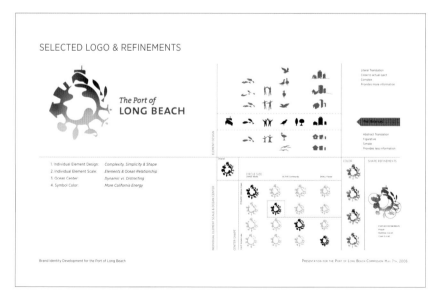

SELECTED LOGO & REFINEMENTS

The Port of
LONG BEACH

1. Individual Element Design: *Complexity, Simplicity & Shape*
2. Individual Element Scale: *Elements & Ocean Relationship*
3. Ocean Center: *Dynamic vs. Distracting*
4. Symbol Color: *More California Energy*

Brand Identity Development for the Port of Long Beach

Presentation for the Port of Long Beach Commission May 7th, 2008

TRAVEL & TOURISM

The travel category covers both destinations and the means of reaching them. It can be a real challenge to sum up all the qualities and attractions of a place in a logo; the best designers succeed by identifying one or two key ideas about the place and capturing their essence in visual form, alluding also to the general atmosphere or spirit of the locale. As for getting there, the old adage about the journey being the goal applies in logo design as well.

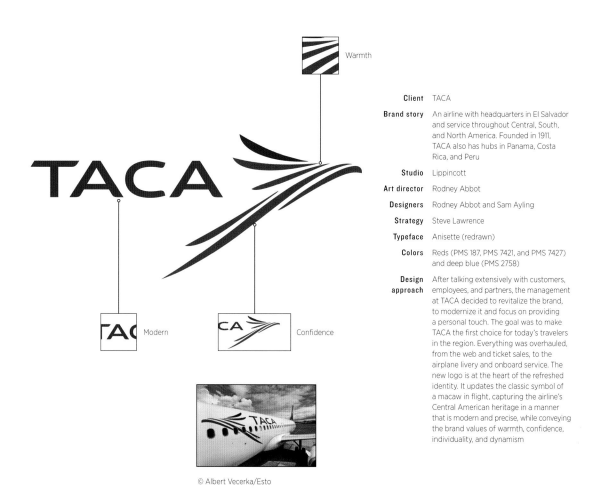

Warmth

Modern

Confidence

© Albert Vecerka/Esto

Client TACA

Brand story An airline with headquarters in El Salvador and service throughout Central, South, and North America. Founded in 1911, TACA also has hubs in Panama, Costa Rica, and Peru

Studio Lippincott

Art director Rodney Abbot

Designers Rodney Abbot and Sam Ayling

Strategy Steve Lawrence

Typeface Anisette (redrawn)

Colors Reds (PMS 187, PMS 7421, and PMS 7427) and deep blue (PMS 2758)

Design approach After talking extensively with customers, employees, and partners, the management at TACA decided to revitalize the brand, to modernize it and focus on providing a personal touch. The goal was to make TACA the first choice for today's travelers in the region. Everything was overhauled, from the web and ticket sales, to the airplane livery and onboard service. The new logo is at the heart of the refreshed identity. It updates the classic symbol of a macaw in flight, capturing the airline's Central American heritage in a manner that is modern and precise, while conveying the brand values of warmth, confidence, individuality, and dynamism

Continuity with previous identity

Lively

Client	Trentino
Brand story	A region in northern Italy
Studio	Minale Tattersfield Design Strategy Group
Design	Marcello Minale, Peter Jones, and Valeria Murabito
Typeface	Trentino Sans
Colors	Blues and greens (process colors)
Design approach	The brief from the tourism authority was to make the brand compete against nearby regions to attract tourism year-round. The existing logo had a somewhat cold feel and didn't convey all that Trentino has to offer the visitor. To build upon the brand's existing equity, the design team at Minale Tattersfield kept the basic typography and the stylized butterfly, but integrated the two. They placed the letters on different levels to echo the mountains and lowlands of the region; added new colors to show the pastures, lakes, wilderness, and clear skies; and eliminated the box. The new identity, which includes monochrome versions, is much more vibrant and ensures a stronger presence for the brand in all digital and print media

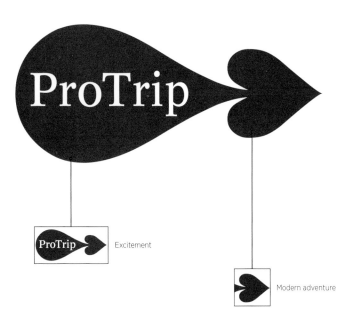

Excitement

Modern adventure

Client	ProTrip
Brand story	A web-based travel agency in the Czech Republic
Studio	Lavmi
Designer	Babeta Ondrová
Typeface	Times Roman
Color	Magenta (process color)
Design approach	The client had no particular requirements for the design of this logo other than that it be unique and visually distinguishable from other travel agencies competing for customers on the web. The designers sought a combination of shape and color that would appear fresh and catch people's attention, while avoiding the usual clichés of the travel business. The combination of symbol and bright color call to mind several desirable associations at once: an arrow points to a choice destination; lips and a speech bubble suggest word-of-mouth recommendations; and a playing-card symbol suggests a fun-filled holiday, and a romantic encounter

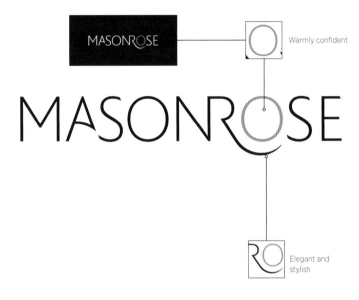

Warmly confident

Elegant and stylish

Client	Mason Rose
Brand story	A company that markets high-end hotels around the world to customers in the UK
Studio	Inaria
Creative directors	Debora Berardi and Andy Bain
Designer	Andy Bain
Typeface	Bespoke
Colors	Deep burgundy (PMS 5115) and rose (PMS 218)
Design approach	Inaria began by articulating the core idea of the Mason Rose brand to give direction to the designers, who then crafted a sophisticated wordmark that captures its most important attributes: trustworthy, intelligent, dynamic, stylish, confident, discerning... A combination of specially modified fine letterforms and an unusual color palette results in a logo, augmented by other brand identity elements, that conveys those values to its audience subtly, but distinctively

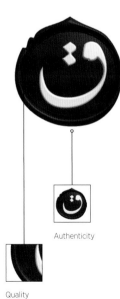

Authenticity

Quality

Client	Qatar Tourism and Exhibitions Authority (QTA)
Brand story	A government agency promoting tourism and trade fairs in the Gulf nation
Studio	Fitch
Art director	Steve Burden
Designer/ Typographer	Shaghig Anserlian
Typefaces	English: Palatino; Arabic: bespoke
Colors	Deep burgundy and gray
Design approach	The QTA sought a new identity to project the same values identified for the country itself: authenticity, quality, and hospitality. The image of a wax seal captures the heritage of Qatar, while the simplified Arabic letterform represents the name. The color scheme reinforces the values: the deep, rich purple connotes royal hospitality, the gentle gray an understated authority. The modern, serif typeface is familiar to a business audience and conveys quality and reliability. The result is a strong, compact, legible identity that is easy to reproduce across a range of formats and media wherever the brand is encountered

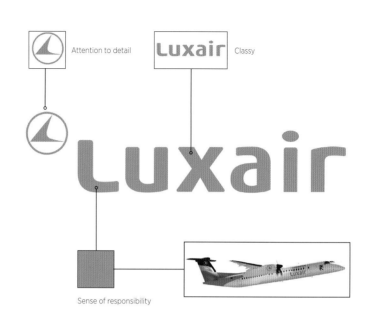

Attention to detail

Classy

Sense of responsibility

Client Luxair

Brand story After years of budget cuts, the national airline of Luxembourg was perceived as old-fashioned and below average in quality and price

Studio Minale Tattersfield Design Strategy Group

Design team Jim Waters and Gwenael Hanquet

Typeface Luxarine (custom typeface based on Dax)

Color Turquoise (PMS 314)

Design approach After an audit of the corporate culture and brand implementation, the design team set about updating the Luxair identity, overhauling its typographic style while retaining the color and modifying the icon only subtly. Changing to a lowercase name and repositioning the circular icon projects a more modern, dynamic feel. The result was applied to aircraft livery, uniforms, airport counters, tickets, websites, and hundreds of other applications, and the new identity was infused into the company culture

Balanced and stable

African

Client Nigerian Eagle Airlines

Brand story After the end of a partnership with Virgin, the national carrier needed a new brand to mark its return to its Nigerian roots and position the brand as the airline of choice for West African travelers

Studio Interbrand Sampson

Designer Anton Krugel

Typeface Bespoke

Colors Green (PMS 3485), yellow (PMS 116), red (PMS 485), and black

Design approach Early solutions revolved around the Nigerian wordmark, with an eagle as a symbol. Interbrand had a different take on the literal eagle, because the icon would compete in an industry full of eagle icons, and it could hold the brand back in the future. A unique mark that would arouse curiosity and inspire pride was needed. Using patterns and colors from the rich, proudly worn clothes of the region, the logo achieves this goal. Its symmetry, in conjunction with the bold wordmark, imparts an inherent feeling of stability and safety to the new airline

Exclusive

Rich

Client	The Valley Club
Brand story	A private golf club in Sun Valley, Idaho, USA
Studio	Mary Hutchison Design
Designer	Mary Chin Hutchison
Typefaces	Garamond Book (adjusted weight) and Interstate Bold
Colors	Dark green (PMS 561) and gold (PMS 8021)
Design approach	The original logo for this invitation-only golf club was designed by the developer, who used the same logo for all his other clubs. Being more exclusive, the Valley Club needed its own logo, but keeping the original colors in order to maintain the brand connection. The new logo draws on topographical features of Sun Valley—the two mountain peaks—for an exclusive image of traditional elegance

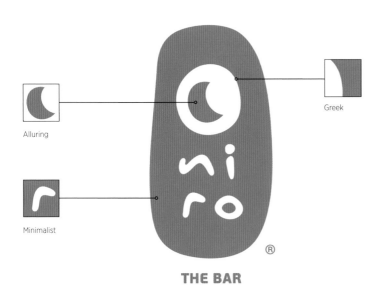

Alluring

Greek

Minimalist

Client	Oniro The Bar
Brand story	An upscale bar in Mykonos, Greece, operated by Zisimopoulou Stamatia
Studio	Chris Trivizas	Design
Art director	Chris Trivizas
Designer	Katerina Kotti
Typeface	Bespoke
Color	Blue (PMS 2925)
Design approach	Mykonos is a busy tourist area with many upscale bars, so Oniro needed a unique identity to help it stand out. The rounded, slightly wobbly form of the logo is inspired partly by the rock used extensively on the premises, partly by the magnificent night-time views the venue affords. The blue and white denote summer holidays in the Greek islands, while the stacked arrangement of the letters alludes to the moonlight shimmering on the water and suggests a nighttime escape. The minimalist look appeals to the cultivated audience

Client	Cooper Square Hotel
Brand story	A boutique hotel in downtown New York City
Studio	//Avec
Designers	Camillia BenBassat, David O'Higgins, and sine elemental
Typeface	Linotype Univers
Color	Black
Design approach	This design envisions the hotel as a frame in which the "creative set" (visitors who are interested in the arts, drama, and music) can converge in a space that reflects their sensibilities. The contrast between the heavy square and the fine lines crisscrossing it sets up a visual tension that captures the ethos of downtown New York, where the wealthy share space with the dispossessed, and cultural sophistication comes into contact with the gritty streets. The absence of color or type from the logo underscores the coolness of the downtown brand

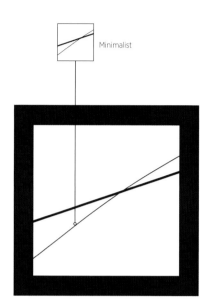

Minimalist

Client	Cresta Hotels
Brand story	A chain of African hotels
Studio	Interbrand Sampson
Designer	Belinda Steenberg
Typeface	Bespoke
Colors	Chrome (PMS 8002) and deep blue (PMS 3025), supplemented with red, yellow, green, and brown
Design approach	Interbrand's first task was to help articulate a set of strategic goals for the brand in a market where resources are strained and brand experience is a vital element in gaining and keeping customers. These strategic points helped the designer define a brand architecture system and made it easier for the company to manage its brands and make the most of their value. The brand's distinctly African essence was expressed through symbolism, texture, pattern, and style, beginning with the new logo, which draws on traditional motifs, but presents them in a modern, world-class style

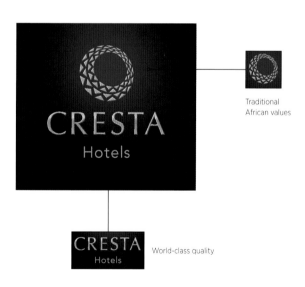

Traditional African values

World-class quality

ONE&ONLY CAPE TOWN

A complex icon that blends cultural influences to convey a richer experience

Brand story Luxury hotel in South Africa

Studio Inaria

Creative director Andrew Thomas

Designers Andrew Thomas and Pablo Basla

Typeface Baskerville (modified)

Colors Dark brown, malachite (PMS 3278), burnt orange, and stone

Design approach Cape Town is dominated by Table Mountain and Signal Hill, and using these landmarks in an identity could have been an obvious cliché. However, research on South African art forms turned up fascinating examples of beadwork and patterns that could be borrowed to create a unique, and uniquely South African, look. The designers began with the idea that Cape Town is a meeting point between Western design precision and the imperfections that make handmade African art so interesting. Applying these principles, they came up with a design that consists of a computer-generated pattern made imperfect by changing or dropping out a few of the "beads." The resulting pattern is at once simple and complex, conveying the beauty and fascination of South Africa. The designers chose to reproduce it using foil blocking, among other techniques, to give it a tactile, craft-like quality when applied to the packaging and luxury gift items the hotel prepares for its guests.

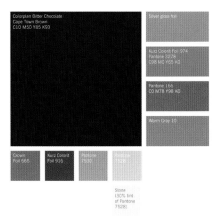

The palette of secondary colors for the brand's graphic identity augments the soft, subtle browns and grays of the logo to create a feeling of understated luxury.

The motif was applied through a complex three-foil print technique. This helps express the tactile quality of handmade art.

To heighten the sense of luxury associated with the brand, special printing techniques, such as foil blocking, were used to craft a richly 3D texture, and a precise, computer-drawn bead pattern was juxtaposed with "handmade" imperfections.

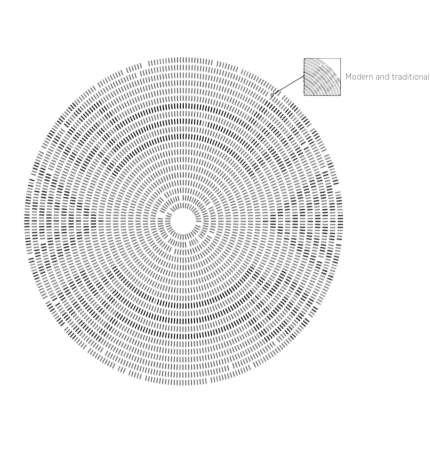

Modern and traditional

The icon is large and versatile enough to use on marketing materials, either whole or as a detail, in a variety of positive or negative color schemes.

CROATIAN NATIONAL TOURIST BOARD

Deploying nearly a dozen language variations to address
an international market audience

Brand story A multilingual visual identity promoting tourism to Croatia,
a Mediterranean country of historic towns and pristine seas

Studio Studio International

Designer Boris Ljubicic

Typeface Handpainted

Colors Yellow (PMS 130), with reds, blues, and green (process colors)

Design approach After gaining independence and rebuilding its infrastructure,
Croatia needed to establish a new identity for itself among
audiences in many different countries, presenting its positive
aspects as a holiday destination.

The logo paints the name in happy, relaxed watercolor strokes, using
bright primary colors. Local-language versions of the country name
are used in each market since the Croatian is unfamiliar to many,
and using solely an English or German version would be politically
difficult and send the wrong message to many tourists.

To unify the many versions, the logo takes advantage of the
coincidence that in most languages, the fourth letter is an A; this
becomes a blue square at the heart of the name, representing the
famously clear sea, with the letter A resembling a sailboat. Above
and to its left is a red square, representing the sun. This also builds
a checkerboard structure, echoing Croatia's heraldic symbolism.

Other letters are embellished with waves or palm fronds, completing
the image of the country as an ideal destination for relaxation. The
resulting identity and its various components are attractive enough
to be creatively applied to towels, bags, apparel, and all manner of
tourist souvenirs, promoting the brand well beyond the traditional
advertising venues.

Using the letter A in the middle of the name as
a visual anchor, the design unifies all the linguistic
versions: English, French, Italian, German, Croatian,
Slovenian, Slovak, Czech, Dutch, and Polish.

Croatian heraldry

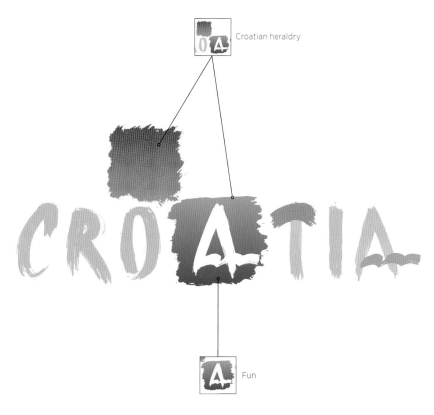

Fun

The red-and-blue checkerboard elicits feelings of summer fun and makes reference both to seaside activities and to Croatia's national heraldry. A full alphabet of hand-painted lettering was crafted to keep all the logo variations consistent.

The logo, or parts of it, can be applied to items such as shopping bags and beach gear in an endless variety of permutations.

SPORTS

People participate in sports to stay healthy, to gain self-esteem, to blow off steam, or simply to have fun. Because of this sports brands, in addition to expressing dynamic movement, usually contain an element of aspiration and speak to our desire for spontaneity, achievement, and self-actualization.

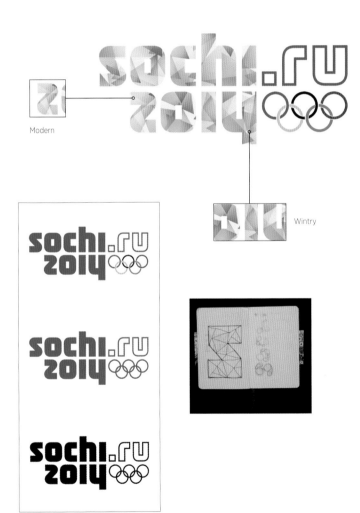

Modern

Wintry

Client	Sochi 2014
Brand story	The Winter Olympics in 2014 will be held in the Russian Black Sea resort of Sochi
Studio	Interbrand
Art director	Christoph Marti
Designers	Alexandra Hulme, Chris Kline, Alexander Kohl, Karen Leong, Anton Stepanenko, Rieko Tsuda, Roman Yershov, and Marco Zimmerli
Typeface	Bespoke
Colors	Mix of blues (PMS 2935 and PMS 286) and cyan (process color) augmented by Olympic colors
Design approach	It is always a matter of great honor and national pride for a country to host the Olympic Games, and always a challenge for designers to balance nationally oriented visual cues with the universal ethos and values of the Games themselves. After experimenting with various ways of communicating Russianness, the designer settled on a solution that combines playful interaction of letters and numerals—four of the characters in the name Sochi are repeated in the year 2014—with a texture that hints at traditional patterns, at the same time suggesting the breathtaking natural beauty of the Russian winter. The inclusion of the famous Olympic rings, a timeless logo whose integrity is closely guarded by the IOC, serves as both brand endorsement and visual adornment, adding a spark of excitement to the cool blues

Exuberance

Heroism

Client Seven Star Soccer

Brand story A seven-a-side soccer league in the UK whose teams of amateur players meet once a week for hour-long games

Studio Imagine-cga

Designer David Caunce

Typeface Commando (modified)

Colors Red, blue, and yellow (process colors based on PMS 185, PMS 300, and PMS 123)

Design approach Although this is an amateur competition, the designer wanted Seven Star Soccer to be an inspirational brand that would boost the feeling of sporting heroism among the players. A crest or shield is a natural emblem for evoking pride, and the prominent 7 emphasizes the difference from the more usual five-a-side leagues. The logo positions this league as a top choice for amateurs in the area, and all 18 team places were quickly filled after it was introduced

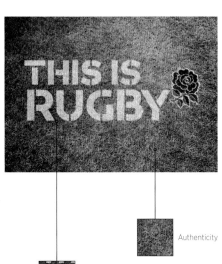

Client This Is Rugby

Brand story The Rugby Football Union, the sport's governing body in England, commissioned a new brand to help recruit people into the sport

Studio Interbrand

Creative directors Andy Howell and Pete Dewar (words)

Typeface Bespoke

Colors Red, white, and grass-green (photographic)

Design approach The brief was to create a brand to promote the core values of England's rugby union: teamwork, discipline, sportsmanship, respect, and enjoyment. This is Rugby was designed to engage audiences from the grass roots up to the elite, and to help newcomers understand what makes rugby special. The design needed to work on rugby balls, gum shields, pitch stencils, beer mats, and online. "This is Rugby" is shorthand for capturing the game's unique character: coaches often give instructions qualified with "because this is rugby"

Authenticity

Camaraderie

Upbeat

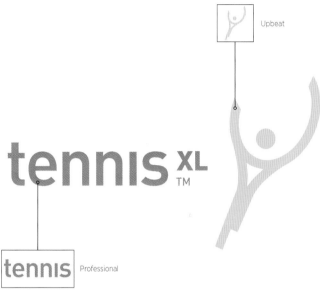

tennis Professional

Client Tennis XL

Brand story An agency running after-school and intensive summertime tennis programs in Vancouver, Canada

Studio Seven25. Design & Typography

Designer Isabelle Swiderski

Typeface DIN

Colors Yellow (PMS 108) and gray (PMS Cool Gray 11)

Design approach The client's challenge was to sell tennis lessons as a way of learning life values: sportsmanship, competitiveness, and play. The identity also needed to appeal to both youths and their parents, who pay for the lessons. The resulting mark—a stylized yellow racquet that doubles as a jumping player—emphasizes the fun and dynamic aspects of the game, while underscoring the importance of the human interaction it enables. Its clean, simple lines and sans-serif typography also convey a crisp professionalism that reassures its audience

Dynamic

Bold and aggressive

Client H+M Racing

Brand story A dirt-bike racing team for youth

Studio Mosaic Creative

Designer Tad Dobbs

Typeface Cosmos Extra Bold

Color Black

Design approach The logo needed to appeal strongly to young boys and to convey the speed and aggressive energy that the sport channels. For inspiration, the designer looked at logos of superhero comics as well as the branding of extreme sporting events. The symbol would have to function without the word-mark in some contexts, such as team apparel, and to work in either black or white depending on the underlying color of the clothing. The logo is sleek and sharp, standing out from other youth teams, and despite its superficial aggressiveness, the symmetry of the mark imparts a sense of balance and self-confidence—important values in youth sports

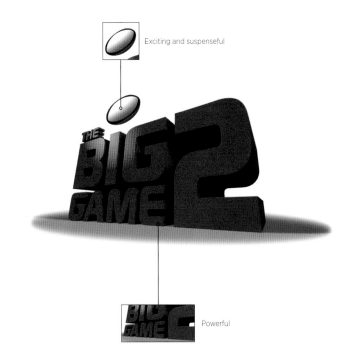

Exciting and suspenseful

Powerful

Client	The Big Game (Harlequins)
Brand story	A London rugby union team needed to promote its post-Christmas match against a main rival; it was moving to a bigger venue and hoping to sell three times the usual number of tickets
Studio	Minale Tattersfield Design Strategy Group
Art director	Marcello Minale
Designer	Giuseppe Mascia
Typeface	Custom-drawn, 3D
Colors	Red, white, and natural colors
Design approach	The visual identity for this heavily promoted sports event speaks in the language of blockbuster entertainment: the looming, heavily shadowed 3D type denotes a heroic spectacle. The branding had to avoid any visual link with the Harlequins' identity so that the event could stand alone and draw the maximum number of spectators. The color and typography therefore build upon the basic values of the rugby union brand, while allowing for yearly updates

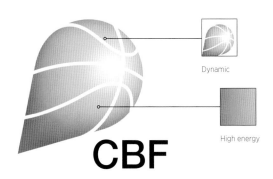

Dynamic

High energy

Client	Czech Basketball Federation
Brand story	The body that governs professional basketball in the Czech Republic sought a new identity after a significant change in its leadership in 2007
Studio	Lavmi
Designer	Babeta Ondrová
Typeface	Helvetica Neue
Colors	Deep blue (PMS 299), red (PMS 485), and orange (PMS 1375)
Design approach	Basketball has a long tradition in the Czech Republic. The new leaders of the federation wanted to indicate the fresh energy they brought to the job by redesigning the organization's identity. The client asked that a classic basketball icon be incorporated into the logo, but a round ball seemed too bland a solution. Instead the designer adapted it to form a new shape that would be representative of the sport, but also sufficiently dynamic to convey some of its energy. This icon has upward movement as it soars toward the basket, and suggests success

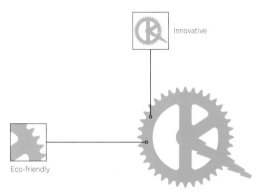

Innovative

Eco-friendly

KILOWATT

BIKES

Client | Kilowatt Bikes

Brand story | An American manufacturer of electric bicycles for casual riders on holidays as well as environment-conscious commuters who don't want to work up a sweat. The flagship model is made of bamboo and carbon fiber

Studio | Starr Tincup

Designer | Tad Dobbs

Typefaces | Delicious Heavy (modified) and Futura Book

Colors | Green (PMS 376) and deep gray (PMS 405)

Design approach | For cost reasons, the brand had to appeal to middle- and upper-class consumers, so the designer turned to brands like Apple for inspiration on how to craft a hip, eco-friendly brand image. The sprocket-and-lightning monogram communicates the essential product unexpectedly and quickly, while the bold type and color combination conveys energy and an Earth-friendly focus

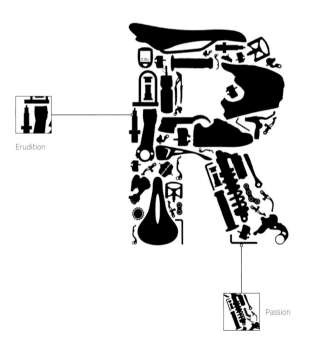

Erudition

Passion

Client | Rock and Road

Brand story | A bicycle store in the UK

Studio | Pencil

Designer | Luke Manning

Typeface | [None]

Color | Black

Design approach | To give the store a distinctive brand that would appeal to cyclists of all levels, from the casual to the expert, the designer crafted a large letter R made up of bicycle parts, including the obvious (seats, pedals, brake handles) and the highly specialized. In some instances, keen cyclists can even spot the manufacturer of a particular part. The result is an original, recognizable brand that communicates the store's expertise and passion for cycling

Openness and togetherness

Approachable, hip, open to all

Client	Community Skate & Snow
Brand story	Store in Arvada, Colorado, USA, selling skateboard and snowboard merchandise. The store aims to change the perception of local skateboard and snowboard stores, emphasizing accessibility and promoting American-made, sustainable products and manufacturers
Studio	Riverbed Design
Designer	Corbet Curfman
Typeface	Bespoke, influenced by Arista 2.0
Colors	Black, with various auxiliary colors
Design approach	The store owners wanted to communicate the positive core ideas of the industry, so the designer came up with a logo that uses line and shape to connect all the elements, suggesting openness and togetherness. The new look attracts a young, hip audience including those new to boarding. Details show variety and individuality, and color variations allow maximum versatility in the retail store

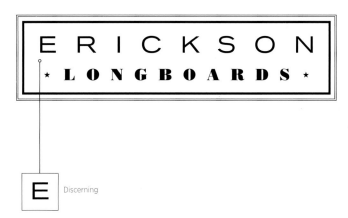

Discerning

Client	Erickson Longboards
Brand story	An American maker of handcrafted skateboard decks from fallen maple and cherry trees
Studio	Think Studio, NYC
Art directors	John Clifford and Herb Thornby
Typefaces	Berthold Akzidenz Grotesk Extended and Bodoni Poster
Color	Black
Design approach	The handcrafting process and the use of found woods result in each board being unique and beautiful. The company wanted an identity that would reflect the product's appeal to design-oriented customers, so the logo has an understated look that adds credibility and a feeling of longstanding pedigree to this new brand

ODSAL SPORTS VILLAGE (OSV)

A simple idea, well executed, with a feeling of spontaneity and energy that reflects its audience's aspirations

Brand story A major redevelopment in Bradford, England, to improve facilities in connection with the London 2012 Olympic Games

Studio Bulletpoint Design

Designer Paul Kerfoot

Typeface Avenir

Colors Multihued, from red-orange to purple-blue

Design approach After many years of similar, failed sports schemes to revitalize the city of Bradford, the 2012 Olympics provided crucial impetus and the necessary investment. The plan, which is focused on Odsal Stadium (home of rugby's Bradford Bulls) and includes spaces for indoor and outdoor sports, a jogging trail, and a pool, also incorporates education, entertainment, health, and accommodation facilities. The development will continue to benefit athletes in the area—professional and amateur, young and old—long after the Games are over.

One of the handicaps faced by previous schemes was the lack of a convincing brand idea or a compelling visual identity. The OSV solution addresses that, and provides both the organizers and the population of Bradford with something they can relate to and pin their hopes and dreams on. In effect, the new logo unifies those working on the scheme and gives direction to their energies. It is simple and direct: a calligraphic figure in an athletic pose, reminiscent of past Olympic identities, with a brilliant added twist—turning the logo 90° reveals the initials OSV. The idea sprang from a moment's inspiration. Testing elicited positive reactions from the client and various groups with a stake in the project.

To complete the visual concept, the strokes are made up of multicolored red-orange and purple-blue gradations that denote the thermal signature of body heat emitted during physical activity. These color blends are then broken down to form sub-brand logos for different components of the development.

The stylized figure of a person running becomes, with a slight tilt of the head, the initials OSV. The sense of energy in motion is heightened by the dynamic coloration of the logo, which resembles the thermal patterns of body heat.

The logo works well in monochrome and also without its typography. A successful logo concept should still be able to work without color or type.

Optimistic

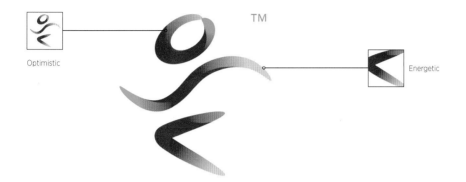

TM

Energetic

ODSAL SPORTS VILLAGE

ODSAL
SPORTS
VILLAGE

HEALTH

ODSAL
SPORTS
VILLAGE

EDUCATION

ODSAL
SPORTS
VILLAGE

ENTERTAINMENT

ODSAL
SPORTS
VILLAGE

ACCOMMODATION

Although preparing a multicolor logo with subtle gradations is easy for printed items like brochures, it is a more complex matter for applications such as embroidered stitching. Fortunately, computer technology makes it achievable without too much trial and error.

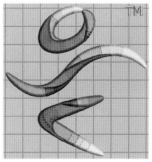

TM

MEDIA & ENTERTAINMENT

We live in a society in which the media—web and video, TV and radio, newspapers and magazines, billboards, and even good old-fashioned books—are becoming more pervasive than ever. As different kinds of media producers and distributors fight to survive in a rapidly evolving media ecology, their brand identities must also push to stay relevant, noticed, and appreciated.

Playful and independent-minded

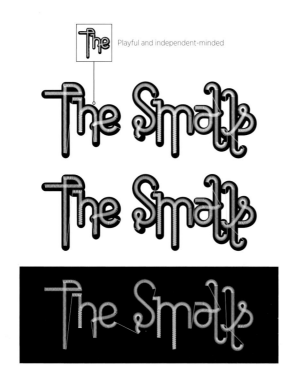

Client	The Smalls
Brand story	A curator of independent short films in the UK that aims to pair raw talent with big broadcasters. The firm organizes awards and is evolving into an online community for people in filmmaking and broadcasting
Studio	Transfer Studio
Designers	Valeria Hedman and Falko Grentrup
Typeface	Bespoke
Color	Yellow (PMS 114)
Design approach	Building on the wordplay of "smalls," which means short film, but also small clothing or underwear, the identity inspires a sense of playfulness with ideas. It is meant, primarily, to catch the attention of independent filmmakers, and also to work across a variety of media. The Smalls has expanded into comedy and is turning into a popular online social network for filmmakers and others in the field, and the designers have continued to work with them on these new projects adding a spark of excitement

Client	Imminent
Brand story	An urban culture magazine in Poland
Studio	InsaneFacilities
Designer	Jarek Berecki
Typeface	Bespoke
Color	Black
Design approach	The magazine wanted a design for their cover nameplate that would focus on the passing of time and make a statement that the demise of humanity is imminent. The designer chose to work with an icon of a mushroom cloud. The grim allusion is softened by the cartoon-like style in which it is rendered, capturing the sly, irreverent attitude of the magazine's audience. The "hipster" typeface completes the effect

Irreverent

Hip

Client	Cherie Smith JCCGV Jewish Book Festival
Brand story	A Jewish-themed cultural event in Vancouver, Canada
Studio	Seven25. Design & Typography
Creative director	Isabelle Swiderski
Designer	Jaime Barrett
Typeface	Apex Sans
Color	Black
Design approach	The organizers sought to convey that the event was inclusive, relevant, and growing. By choosing a simple visual approach, the designer was able to position the organization as proactive. The icon combines the ideas of an open book and a menorah, symbols that are widely recognized and associated with the Jewish faith, but not explicitly religious. Its upward thrust, combined with the clean, simple typography, convey the organizers' values and position the event in the desired way

CHERIE SMITH JCCGV

JEWISH
BOOK FESTIVAL

Growth and inclusiveness

Timeless typography

Modernist

CHRISTOPHER B. SMITH
RAFAEL
FILM CENTER

Glamorous

Client	Rafael Film Center
Brand story	A cinema in California dedicated to showing classic and independent film
Studio	MINE
Art director	Christopher Simmons
Designer	Tim Belonax, updated by Christopher Simmons
Typefaces	Bespoke, combined with Gotham
Color	Orange (PMS 152)
Design approach	MINE was hired to design three logos for related projects: the Mill Valley Film Festival, marking its 30th year; the Rafael Film Center, which hosts the festival; and the parent organization, the California Film Institute. The three identities had to work together, so they needed to be stylistically connected. The classic neon signage on the Film Center building provided a starting point for this logo, which is an update of an original design by Mark Fox. It captures the excitement of going to a picture show, without resorting to clichéd devices such as a film projector or film itself

West Coast
(USA) ethos

CALIFORNIA
FILM INSTITUTE

Client	California Film Institute
Brand story	A membership organization dedicated to showing films and educating the public about film
Studio	MINE
Art director	Christopher Simmons
Designer	Tim Belonax
Typefaces	Bespoke, combined with Gotham
Color	Blue (PMS 549)
Design approach	This identity works together with those for the Rafael Film Center and the Mill Valley Film Festival. Like the former, the logo derives its lettershapes from the neon signage on the exterior of the Rafael Film Center. By focusing on stylizing the initial letters, the designers were able to sidestep the common visual clichés of film and create a recognizable mark that nonetheless connotes the cinematic experience

Timeless

Client	Mill Valley Film Festival
Brand story	An annual film festival in California
Studio	MINE
Art directors	Christopher Simmons
Designer	Tim Belonax
Typeface	Gotham Rounded
Color	Light green (PMS 390)
Design approach	For the 30th anniversary of this event, the designers were asked to come up with a new logo that would communicate the love of film that is at the heart of every such festival. The resulting icon resists the usual symbology of film festival logos in favor of the highly stylized initials MV, topping them off with a little heart formed by the intersection of the two shortest lines. The mark carefully follows the line thickness and proportions of its sister marks, the California Film Institute and Rafael Film Center, to ensure that the three logos are visually integrated and can work together well

Enthusiastic

Erudite

Client	Greek Film Center
Brand story	A Film Center that aims its "art" films at a more sophisticated audience than the average cinema
Studio	Chris Trivizas | Design
Designer	Chris Trivizas
Typeface	PF Highway Sans Pro
Color	Black
Design approach	The main inspiration for this logo is the cinema itself with its rows of plush seats leading down to the silver screen. The minimal style in which they are rendered, together with the lack of color, is intended to catch the attention of upscale audiences and allude to older, black-and-white films of a certain status and quality

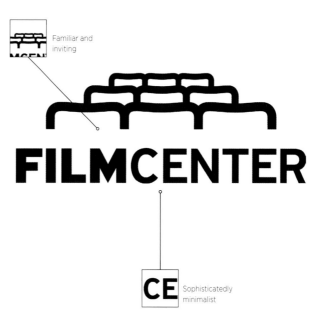

Familiar and inviting

Sophisticatedly minimalist

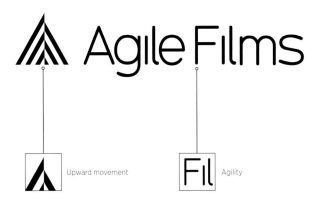

Client	Agile Films
Brand story	A film-production company that makes commercials, animations, online video, music video, and other moving images
Studio	Studio EMMI
Designer	Emmi Salonen
Typeface	Rounded sans serif (not specified)
Color	Black
Design approach	The design is based on the upward arrow shape of the initial letter: the sense of movement suggested by the alternating stripes gives a feeling of movement toward a peak, reinforcing the high-end quality of the work, while also connoting the lines of a video-screen image. The light, slightly rounded letterforms convey the idea of a firm that is nimble and responsive, as its name implies. The logo captures the ethos of the company so well it was used as a guiding motif for the interior design of Agile Films' new offices

Upward movement

Agility

Client	Oro Pagalvés
Brand story	A creative video studio in Lithuania
Designer	Tadas Karpavicius
Typeface	Gagaille seconde
Color	Black
Design approach	The studio works in a variety of media, producing animation and other works. The name translates into English as "air bag," so the designer chose a surreal combination of wings and a pillow for the logo. The somewhat grungy, hand-drawn lettering, with filled-in counters and a tilted baseline, gives an impression of stark creativity and an underground sensibility, while the logo as a whole is perfectly clear and accessible, even friendly

Whimsical

Handmade

Client	Alex Coletti Productions
Brand story	TV production company, started by a man born and bred in Brooklyn, New York City
Studio	Think Studio, NYC
Designers	John Clifford and Herb Thornby
Typeface	Trade Gothic
Colors	Blue (PMS 650) and brown (PMS 462)
Design approach	The client's main concern was that the logo look great when it appears briefly on screen at the end of a show. His pride in his Brooklyn heritage was incorporated into the logo in a way that is instantly recognizable, but avoids looking trite. The chosen silhouette, shot from a stark angle on Brooklyn Bridge itself, conjures the cinematographic qualities of this icon and captures the bold, confident feeling of the borough. When it is broadcast, the squares twinkle and change color, using a modern, stylish palette. "The client often lets me know about the compliments he receives for this logo," says John Clifford

Slick

alex coletti
productions

Current

Client	Banana Split Productions
Brand story	Television production agency based in London
Studio	Fivefootsix
Typeface	Franklin Gothic (modified)
Colors	Yellow (PMS 116) and brown (PMS 4625)
Design approach	Given the somewhat humorous name of this company, using a banana in a visual way was unavoidable. By turning it into a typographic symbol (or, to be precise, turning a typographic symbol into a banana), the designers were able to bring out the company's playful personality in a versatile form, and to move conceptually beyond the earlier logo, which pictured a half-peeled banana. The parentheses can be adapted to almost any context, making the banana icon part of the language the brand uses. In this regard, the logo itself becomes corollary to the contextual uses of the banana/parenthesis elsewhere in the company's communications

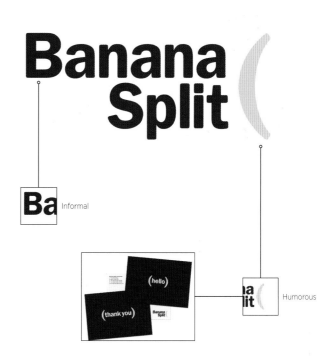

Banana
Split

Informal

(hello)

(thank you)

Humorous

Client	Rock Zone
Brand story	A music publisher
Studio	Ambient
Designer	Scott Mosher
Typeface	Impact
Colors	Red, yellow, and black (process colors)
Design approach	The company needed a bold logo to use on book covers and other branded materials that would convey the powerful feelings of rock music and appeal to an audience reared on Web 2.0 graphics. The combination of a strong font and aggressive colors captures the young, rebellious spirit of the brand's target market

Energetic

Wild

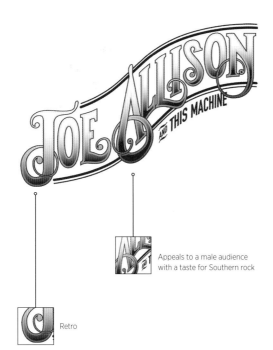

Client	Joe Allison and This Machine
Brand story	Alternative country music band from the Dallas area of Texas, USA, whose music has a retro-style, Southern-rock feel
Studio	Creative Squall
Designer/ Typographer	Tad Dobbs
Typefaces	Bespoke (Joe Allison) and DIN Engshrift (This Machine)
Colors	Red (PMS 1807), yellow (PMS 726), and brown (PMS 4625)
Design approach	The designer took inspiration from the prevalent styles of album-cover artwork of the 1960s and early 1970s when major-label bands tended to have consistent logos to identify their releases. This logo is a nod to the artwork of the Allman Brothers in particular, and to the typography of older posters for carnival showmen and traveling magicians in general. The final logo needed to be strong enough to use on the debut album cover, and flexible enough for use on T-shirts, posters, stickers, and on the web

Appeals to a male audience with a taste for Southern rock

Retro

Well-traveled

Weathered

Client Lies That Rhyme

Brand story A music publisher based in Nashville, Tennessee, USA

Studio Clay McIntosh Creative

Designer Clay McIntosh

Typefaces Selections from the Wild West Press collection by Walden Font, including Cut and Shoot, Royal Nonesuch, Shelldrake, Wildwash, Ashwood Condensed, Stockton, Ashwood Extra Bold, and Gatlin Bold

Colors Red (PMS 188), tan (PMS 153), and brown (PMS 4625)

Design approach The aim was to create a mark that stands out and calls for attention, with more visual impact than its competitors. It needed to project a mature, experienced, but fun-loving image to the Nashville music business; the name, the circus-poster typefaces, and the fading colors indicate all these things

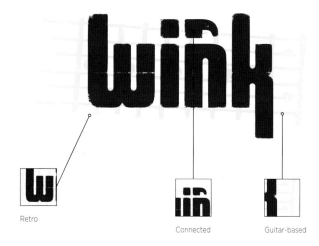

Retro

Connected

Guitar-based

Client Wink

Brand story Classic-rock cover band from Alaska, USA

Studio The Whole Package

Designer/ Typographer Leila Singleton

Typeface Bespoke

Colors Deep blue (PMS 281) and yellow (PMS 108)

Design approach 1970s type styles were the inspiration for this custom logotype, and the letterforms were distressed to get a vintage look, inspired by worn LP covers. The logotype and guitar-inspired background texture tell the observant viewer a bit about the band's sound; however, to give it a contemporary resonance, the dot on the "i," a rotated semicolon, references online communication. There was no color choice—the band fancied a logo in blue and yellow

Underground

Independent

Client   Klaipeda Goes Indie

Brand story   Indie rock music event in Klaipeda, Lithuania

Designer   Tadas Karpavicius

Typeface   Chinese Rocks

Color   Black

Design approach   This logo perfectly matches the aesthetic of its audience and the subject it represents: independent, noncommercial rock music on the fringes of Europe. The history of the interplay between graphic design and rock music is a long one, and this identity ties into it well. It captures the creative tension and breaking of bounds embodied by the music, while giving expression to the individuality and nonconformism of its audience. Nevertheless, its relatively simple form and lack of color make it suitable for low-resolution applications such as screenprinting onto T-shirts or printing inexpensive posters

 Electronic and retro 80s

Client   TRON

Brand story   A monthly techno and electro club event in Malmö, Sweden

Studio   Nils-Petter Ekwalls Illustrationsbyrå

Designer   Nils-Petter Ekwall

Typeface   Bespoke

Colors   Multicolored blend

Design approach   This was a new club concept from Staffan and Niklas Ehrlin who had run music clubs before, but wanted something a bit more "old school" and exclusive with this project. "Tron" is Swedish for faith or belief and the Ehrlins are among the last keepers of the flame for the techno movement in southern Sweden. They wanted a logo that looked like it had been produced in 1982 (the year the Disney film *Tron* was released) and they liked neon. The designer was inspired by sci-fi films from the early 1980s and Italo disco record sleeves. He also studied the graphics for the movie *Tron* to avoid inadvertent infringement of its design

Distraction

Visual noise

Client	Arm The Lonely
Brand story	An independent platform for alternative music composed and performed in banal surroundings
Designer	Alexander Egger
Typeface	Bespoke
Color	Light turquoise (PMS 566)
Design approach	Arm The Lonely (the name is a reference to a Savoy Grand song) is an Austrian label that aims to offer a critical reflection on pop culture and consumerism, with a philosophical and polemical approach to music. Its activities include performances, art exhibitions, and publishing. The designer aimed to capture the idea of sound as noise in a deliberate context. Using found footage, scratches, photocopies, and visual noise, he came up with a logo whose exact appearance changes with each context and each low-budget, DIY means of applying it: stamped, cut out, sprayed on, or projected

Pixelated

Video game–inspired

Client	Technique
Brand story	A drum 'n' bass music event in Poland
Studio	Insane Facilities
Designer	Jarek Berecki
Typeface	Quer
Color	Black
Design approach	The musicians taking part in this event used sounds in their music sets that were characteristic of the 8-bit gaming platforms of the early 1980s, such as Pac-Man and Space Invaders. The designer decided to capitalize on the obvious visual associations of such sounds and come up with a complex mark that breaks many of the traditional rules of logo design, incorporating borrowed illustrations and text to become, in effect, a self-contained poster. The result is a unique and memorable symbol that reminds its audience of the event's atmosphere

Mechanical

Rhythmic

Client	Promophobia
Brand story	An electronic music label and music-production company based in Lithuania
Designer	Tadas Karpavicius
Typeface	Relish Gargler
Color	Black
Design approach	The designer let the music itself be the inspiration for the design of this logo. Electronic music is usually based on repeating rhythms and tonal intervals, so the chosen lettershapes are severely geometric and impart a mechanical, repetitive feel in keeping with the genre. The lack of color keeps the focus on the forms. The tilted P in a circle hints at the spinning vinyl disks that are a DJ's métier, and provides an iconic variant of the logo to use in smaller or simpler applications

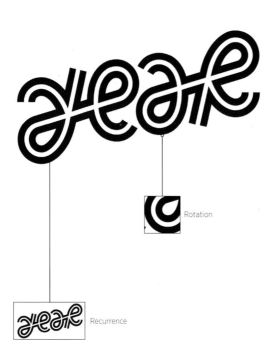

Rotation

Recurrence

Client	YEAR
Brand story	A regular DJ event in which each evening focuses on a single year from the period 1956 to 2006
Studio	MINE
Designers	Christopher Simmons and Tim Belonax
Typeface	Bespoke
Color	Black
Design approach	The idea of playing songs from just one year all night long was the inspiration for this mark, in which the same form, inverted, comprises the second half of the word so that "year" can be read upside-down as well as right-side-up. This hints at the spinning vinyl records as well as the idea of recapturing the feelings of one's youth. At the same time, the cursive forms have an upbeat, California-style feel and are simple enough to work on signs, labels, T-shirts, and many other applications

Client	Ich Robot
Brand story	A small nightclub in Malmö, Sweden, for minimal synth and electro music enthusiasts
Studio	Nils-Petter Ekwalls Illustrationsbyrå
Designer	Nils-Petter Ekwall
Typeface	Bespoke
Color	Black
Design approach	The club owner wanted an identity that would give expression to the melancholy and hardness of the music in an "old-school, science-fiction, or futuristic kind of way." Seeking inspiration, Ekwall searched through old graphic magazines from the 1920s and 1930s, and everything he could find that was related to the Metropolis/ Fritz Lang/1920s futuristic feel. The image of a robot is almost synonymous with the synth/electro genre of music—many refer to it as "robot music"—and its combination with the unlikely symbol of a pentagram results in a strong, memorable logo

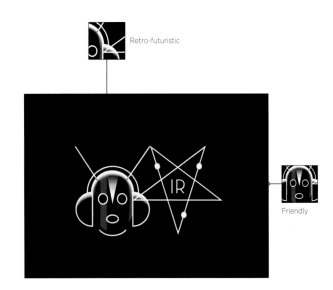

Retro-futuristic

Friendly

Client	Team Dank
Brand story	Concert and event promotions and productions company
Designer	Colin Decker
Typeface	Bespoke
Colors	Purple blending to red/magenta
Design approach	The designer aimed to create a logo that reflected the company's passion for outdoor music festivals, jam bands, and all things environmentally conscious and friendly. "A happy musical tree that's high on life," is how Decker describes it. He looked back to the organic, hand-lettered type on 1970s concert posters from the legendary Fillmore club and came up with a "fun, funky musical tree." The symbol clearly speaks to the style of the music and to the social and political values of the brand's customers. A stripped-down version was also created, for use in different contexts

Gregarious

Psychedelic

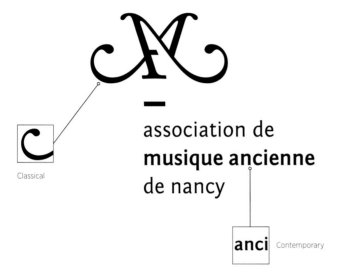

Classical

Contemporary

association de
musique ancienne
de nancy

Client Association de Musique Ancienne
de Nancy

Brand story An organization promoting medieval,
Renaissance, and baroque music in
Nancy, France

Studio Studio Punkat

Designer Hugo Roussel

Typefaces Caslon (monogram) and Fontin Sans

Color Black

Design approach The organization wanted an identity that
would clearly denote early classical music
while avoiding the outdated visual clichés
common to classical music programs so it
could distinguish itself from competitors.
The designer crafted a monogram from
the initials MA, inspired by the *Book of
Hours*, that is at once classical and modern,
suggesting the musicians' gestures and
the curves of the instruments. Combining
an eighteenth-century and a twenty-first-
century typeface completes the effect; the
illustrative style used on the organization's
posters and fliers is likewise a postmodern
collage of the old and the new

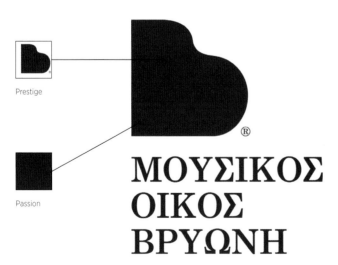

Prestige

Passion

Client Vrionis Music House

Brand story A music store serving an upmarket
clientele in Greece

Studio Chris Trivizas | Design

Designer Chris Trivizas

Typeface PF Century

Color Burgundy (PMS 519)

Design approach In the Greek alphabet, the first letter of
the name Vrionis is Beta, which happens
to resemble the outline of a grand piano.
This association elevates the brand and
lends it an air of prestige. The minimalism
of the icon, combined with a sturdy serif
font, communicates confidence and
sophistication, while the purple conveys
the firm's charm and passion for music

Transcends local and cultural barriers

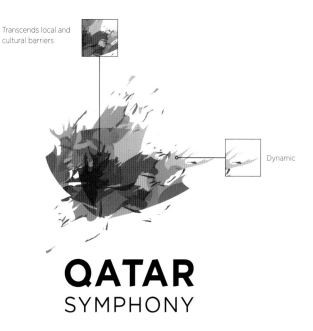

Dynamic

Client	Qatar Symphony
Brand story	An 80-member orchestra whose classical performances tell of the achievements of the state of Qatar. It was established by the Qatar Foundation to celebrate music as common to all civilizations
Studio	Fitch
Art director	David Walker
Designer/ Typographer	Hammad Iqbal
Typeface	Bespoke
Colors	Purple, mauve, and sand
Design approach	To visualize the symphony orchestra and its music, the designer reflected Qatari heritage using color and forms that capture a sense of movement. The new identity needed to look modern, yet retain a local, traditional touch. The result blends in limitless ways to convey a sense of transcending boundaries, both geographic and cultural

QATAR
SYMPHONY

Client	NKD (Neva Killa Dream)
Brand story	A South African band developed a program to prevent drug use by disadvantaged or abused children, and subsequently adopted the program brand as the band's identity
Agency	Interbrand Sampson
Art director	Anton Krugel
Director	Jacqueline Sampson
Typeface	Stencil
Colors	Magenta and black (process colors)
Design approach	The band's name, NKD, comes from the initials of the members' names. When the band wanted to develop and champion their anti-drug program, they called it Neva Killa Dream and asked Interbrand's designers for an identity to use in securing sponsorship from a global electronics company. After the success of that effort, the band took on the identity itself. The stylized black swan represents the beauty of life and the desire to fulfill one's hopes and dreams; the distressed spray-graffiti style, with a giant teardrop (or drop of blood), evokes the pathos of a young life destroyed by drugs.

Pathos

Streetwise

STORIES: PROJECTS IN FILM

Modernist design allows a flexible, modular program to be built for a range of logo applications

Brand story A film-production company specializing in youth and community film projects, based on strong narratives with a social message

Designer Tom Munckton

Typeface Akzidenz Grotesk Roman

Colors Greens (PMS 3415 and PMS 3405) and yellow (PMS 3965)

Design approach The logo is an abstract representation of the pages of a storybook meeting at the spine. Enclosing this symbol within an "undrawn" circle suggests a couple of thoughts: that these stories are a microcosm of life's larger stories, and that the act of storytelling can occur in all media, including film. The overall style of the identity recalls the functionalism of earlier decades, underscoring the realist, documentary nature of the subject.

Like most conventional logos, this one works just as well in black-and-white as in color, and augmented by its carefully arranged name as it does alone.

Accompanying the basic logo design is a set of specifications for other aspects of the complete visual identity, including specific colors and typography, and examples of a layout style. These are laid out in a brand guideline poster that doubles as a reference for the client and a statement of intent for potential clients.

Although the logo idea is fairly simple, its graphic execution is detailed enough that reproduction at very small sizes could be problematic, with the lines becoming too fine to "read" properly. To help the logo function at small sizes, the designer created an alternate version using fewer lines, getting the idea across without compromising on clarity. The specifications give the exact size threshold for switching from one version to the other—45mm.

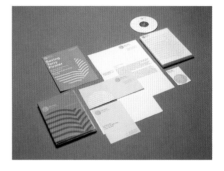

Using a limited color palette saves money, but requires a brand mark that is bold and distinctive so that its printed materials don't look tiresome.

Denotative

Cohesive

Stories
Projects in Film

Stories
Projects in Film

The designer prepared two versions of the logo: a primary one and a version for use at smaller sizes. The small version differs primarily in the number of lines within the circle; having fewer lines prevents them from appearing too fine to give the correct impression.

The logo can work as a strong central visual device as well as a background pattern. This is important since many of the organization's materials couldn't show images from a specific film project.

FALCO INVERNALE RECORDS

A logo made the old-fashioned way, to convey a retro sensibility that appeals to a discerning audience

Brand story	A small, independent record label specializing in limited vinyl releases of alternative electronic dance music, run from Toulouse, France, by the artist Philippe Hayet
Studio	Nils-Petter Ekwalls Illustrationsbyrå
Designer	Nils-Petter Ekwall
Typeface	Neutraface Text Italic
Color	Black
Design approach	Most of the music issued by this boutique record label has an early 1980s, somewhat melancholy feel: electro, synth pop, and italo disco. The name is Italian for "winter falcon." The issues are small—300 to 500 per release—and every record is hand numbered. The typical customer is a young, male record collector or DJ from Europe or the USA, with a huge record collection. The client wanted "something dark" for the logo, and it had to work on both web and print, and sometimes one-color prints.

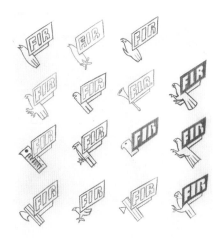

The designer immediately thought of a lasting design with a classic feel that could stand out from the competitors, which normally have very slick "designer music" logos that are cool for 12 months, then look very dated; or have minimalistic or bold techno logos.

The solution was inspired by Italian and German art-deco graphics. The designer went through his packaging collection—mostly art supplies, bottles of drawing ink and stamps—looking for something "stable." There is no literal connection between the bird icon and the company's activities; rather, there is a looser conceptual link between the mood connotations of "winter" and the hard-angled, severe style of the logo.

After making numerous thumbnail sketches, the designer picked the favorites and worked them out with a Japanese brush in india ink and white gouache to avoid the computer feel. He then refined the best design in Illustrator.

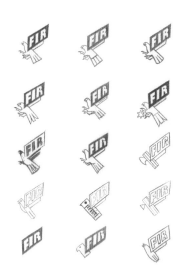

After settling on a basic concept, the designer drew dozens of possible variations to find just the right combination of stylized falcon and boxed initials.

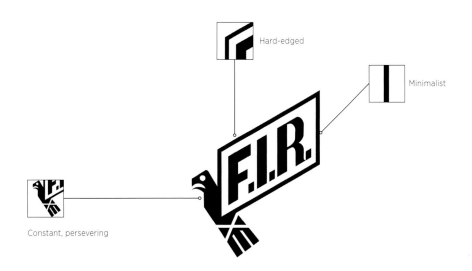

Hard-edged

Minimalist

Constant, persevering

Falco Invernale Records

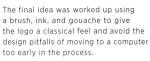

To begin with, the designer explored some of the many ways in which a falcon could be stylized and the initials incorporated into a logo.

The final idea was worked up using a brush, ink, and gouache to give the logo a classical feel and avoid the design pitfalls of moving to a computer too early in the process.

THE NEW YORK TIMES

With only modest changes through 150 years of design evolution, a newspaper brand goes from commonplace to distinguished

Brand story Founded in 1851, this independent newspaper is now printed nationally in the USA, as well as providing weekly supplements to other newspapers around the world; nytimes.com is one of the most popular and innovative news websites in the world

Studio Various

Designer Various

Typeface Bespoke, based on traditional Blackletter or Gothic faces

Color Black

Design approach While the designers of the original nameplate weren't recorded, typographer Matthew Carter, former *New York Times* design director Lou Silverstein, and Pentagram partner Michael Bierut have all worked on adapting and updating the logo.

Among the challenges facing these designers were changes in orthographic style (the hyphen in New-York was dropped in the late nineteenth century, the dot after Times in 1965); changes in technology from metal type to phototypesetting to digital platemaking; by the turn of the twenty-first century, a plethora of new media including magazines, online, mobile, and video; and the novel signage requirements of a new, modern headquarters building near the eponymous Times Square in midtown Manhattan.

The use of Blackletter type for newspaper banners was once so common as to be a cliché. Over the last century, most newspapers have adopted more modern lettering styles and the *Times*, by virtue of being one of a few holdouts, can now claim the style as its own, and by using it in so many modern contexts, it has made the old-fashioned appear timeless.

The banner has been subtly redrawn numerous times to give it a cleaner, more consistent look as part of an overall update to the newspaper's image. The designers have always taken pains to avoid using the gothic style of the banner logo for section heads and other typographic treatments within the paper, preferring to use contrasting styles such as the delicate Cheltenham, modernist Helvetica Bold, or heavy, slab-serif Karnak.

New-York Daily Times.

1850s

The New-York Times.

1860s

The New-York Times.

1890s

The New York Times.

1930s

The New York Times

1960s

The banner or nameplate at the top of the front page traditionally announces the publication on the newsstand as a logo announces a package on a supermarket shelf. *The New York Times*' logo has changed only minimally since the paper was founded in 1851. The most recent update was in the 1980s, by noted type designer Matthew Carter.

The context in which the logo is used has hardly changed from 1851 (left) to 2010 (right), in spite of technological changes such as the daily use of color photographs and cultural changes such as beginning the most important story on the right, rather than the left.

Over the years, *The New York Times*' responses to new media demands have included:

- The capital T was specially adapted to use as a free-standing logo on the cover of "T Styles," a Sunday supplement published several times a year with an accompanying multimedia website.

- Low-resolution pixel versions were developed for small mobile screens.

- The increasing use of web video necessitated an animated version of *The New York Times* banner to serve as an introductory shot.

- International partnerships to publish content from the *Times* in other countries' newspapers has necessitated finding harmonious ways to combine the *Times* logo with graphically diverse banners.

- When the company's new headquarters was opened in 2007, local regulations dictated that building signage be offset from the façade; designers at Pentagram came up with a novel technique, building upon the system of ceramic rods designed by architect Renzo Piano, reconstructing the logo out of thicker black elements placed over the grid of white ones.

To comply with Times Square building regulations, which called for a logo suspended in front of the façade, designers at Pentagram recreated the letterforms using a clever system of horizontal ceramic rods.

In web video titles the logo is animated, with its outline drawn across a blue background and the parts cross-fading with the whole.

  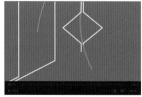 

When *The New York Times* launched its quarterly "T Style" magazine in the mid-2000s, it chose a carefully fattened version of the initial T as the standalone logo for that sub-brand. The newspaper's Wine Club uses an icon in which the swirling wine in the glass also resembles the top of the gothic-style T.

WEB & TELECOMMUNICATIONS

Web and telecom firms are often cutting-edge innovators in areas such as networking and interface development, with advanced ideas about how humans relate to each other and how we use technology to connect to the world. The best identities in this area reflect some element of human interaction, rather than mere technology.

Bold and friendly without being patronizing

Inclusive

Client	Worldeka
Brand story	An online social networking platform for global citizens who aim to change the world, bringing together videoconferencing, educational resources, NGO and charity presence, and information in environmental, developmental, and humanitarian fields
Studio	Landor Associates
Creative directors/ Designers	Jason Little and Mike Staniford
Designers/ Typographers	Joao Peres and Serhat Ferat
Typeface	Bespoke (full identity uses VAG Rounded)
Colors	Magenta and black (process colors)
Design approach	Visually, Worldeka (the name, from Sanskrit, means one world) needed to convey its promise of fostering communication, collaboration, and a sense of belonging to a revolutionary global community. The brand needed to be bold, confident, and uncompromising. The designers embraced the brand idea of collectivity. There is no single Worldeka logo: within the brand framework (the initials WE, the color palette, the personality), users can come up with their own mantras such as "Working Effectively" or "Warriors Embracing." The illustrative logotypes, like miniature posters, form the brand's signature style and express its revolutionary spirit of networking to bring about positive change

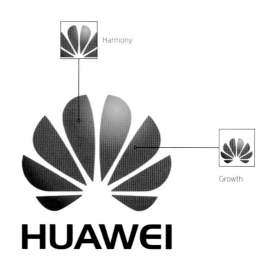

Harmony

Growth

HUAWEI

Client	Huawei
Brand story	Founded in 1989 in Shenzhen, China, the firm is a leader in network technology. Huawei's equipment is used by more than a billion people worldwide
Studio	Interbrand China
Designers	Tim Arrowsmith and Chuan Jiang
Typeface	Bespoke
Colors	Reds (process color blends) and black
Design approach	Huawei wanted a new identity to signal its changes from a local start-up to a world-class brand, and from a technology-focused company to one with an emphasis on customers, innovation, sustainable growth, and traditional Chinese principles of harmony. The new logo reflects an enterprising spirit, but also commitment to helping customers with innovative, competitive services and long-term value. The segments appear to rise symmetrically, giving a sense of peacefulness, while the gradations that give them dimension are focused toward the east, as if reflecting the sunrise

Word of mouth

Inclusive

Client	The Best Of
Brand story	An online business directory allowing customers in cities throughout the UK to give feedback on local companies. Which businesses are listed is determined by word-of-mouth recommendations
Studio	The House
Art director	Steven Fuller
Designer	Andy Gerrard
Typeface	Interstate
Colors	Light blue (PMS 277) and dark blue (PMS 281)
Design approach	Businesses can only appear in the listings if they are really "the best," as judged by customers' comments. The website's identity had to communicate this instantly, and a stylized speech bubble seemed the best way to achieve this. It also has other advantages: being extendable, the lozenge provides a clear system for names to be incorporated (thebestofbath, etc.) as the brand is franchised to other cities and towns. The all-lowercase type makes the identity more friendly and embracing, while legibility is addressed by alternating the colors of the words

Exuberance and
spontaneity

emfesta.
com festas
de portugal

Client	EmFesta.com – Festas de Portugal
Brand story	An online guide to fairs and festivals in Portugal
Studio	Playout
Designer	Tiago Machado
Typeface	Clarendon
Colors	Multicolored, with name in black (PMS 029) and gray (PMS Cool Gray 4)
Design approach	This website is directed at both lovers and organizers of fairs and festivals. The client asked the designer to "surprise us." So he did—with a logo that captures a burst of fireworks, representing the full range and variety of fairs and festivals, without being biased toward one shape or color, or referring specifically to any single region or event

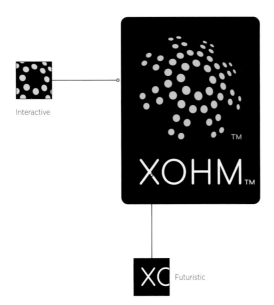

Interactive

Futuristic

Client	Xohm (Sprint Nextel)
Brand story	A nationwide WiMAX wireless broadband network in the USA operated by Sprint. Users can download movies, watch video, and play games on mobile devices at speeds typical of cable networks, without monthly contracts or fees
Studio	Lippincott
Art director	Rodney Abbot
Designers	Rodney Abbot, Peter Chun, and Brendán Murphy
Typeface	Bryant (redrawn)
Colors	Lime green (PMS 382) and black
Design approach	The logo captures the idea of connecting people, places, and devices with a thrilling and attractive icon that alludes to space-age video games. The dots in an asterisk pattern connote zooming in to a target and making contact, and also reinforce the initial X of the name; the radiating lines suggest unlimited freedom of movement

Client	Hayneedle
Brand story	An online shopping site that aims to give customers a broad selection of hard-to-find home and lifestyle products
Studio	Lippincott
Art director	Su Mathews
Designers	Vincenzo Perri, Sam Ayling, Thy Nguyen-Huu, Saki Tanaka, Matt Calkins, and Bogdan Geana
Typeface	ITC Officina Sans
Colors	Multicolored
Design approach	The name and symbol capture the joy of finding a perfect item or gift from a seemingly endless sea of products. The overlapping colored lines represent options and choice; the name is set in a modern, friendly font that conveys the playful aspect of the brand

hayneedle

ha — Friendly

Sense of discovery

Client	Geeknet
Brand story	The parent company of several technology-oriented websites and blogs based in the USA, including Slashdot, ThinkGeek, SourceForge, Ohloh, and freshmeat
Studio	Interbrand
Art director	Kurt Munger
Designers	Kurt Munger and Noriko Ohori
Typeface	Freeway, modified
Color	Black
Design approach	Most Geeknet websites are characterized by a sense of camaraderie among users, who are typically bright, technically adept young people more comfortable with socializing online than in person. Many came of age in an era when computers and video games were commonplace. The logo is reminiscent of characters from vintage arcade games; its arrow-shaped tentacles refer to the multiple ventures under Geeknet's umbrella, the varied interests of its sites' visitors, and the social networking that takes place on the sites

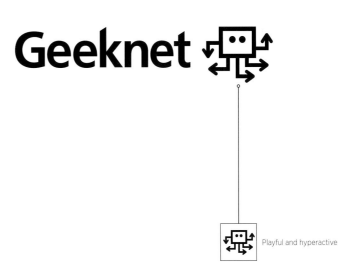

Playful and hyperactive

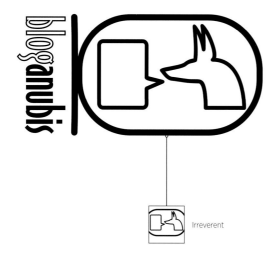

Irreverent

Client	Blog Anubis
Brand story	A blog dealing with plagiarism and the critique of advertising in Kuwait and the Gulf coast states
Studio	Paragon Marketing Communications
Art director	Louai Alasfahani
Designer	Konstantin Assenov
Typeface	Bodega Sans Oldstyle (redrawn)
Color	Black
Design approach	Anubis, the ancient Egyptian messenger god, was often a revealer of truth. He is typically portrayed with a dog's head. Enclosing his silhouette in a cartouche with a speech balloon captures the idea behind the blog and uses gentle humor to appeal to an audience of advertising and marketing professionals in the Gulf region

Accessible and consumer-oriented

Client	Rave
Brand story	Mobile integration for university campuses in the USA
Studio	Siegel+Gale
Creative director	Doug Sellers
Senior designers	Rob Sawitz and Joo Chae
Typeface	Helvetica Neue
Color	Black
Design approach	Although most college students in the USA have some kind of mobile device, many universities weren't able to systematically communicate important information via this channel. Rave wanted to assert its leadership in this emerging area by simplifying its brand story, refreshing its visual identity, and relaunching at universities across the USA. The logo needed to work alongside the school and mobile carrier logos, so Siegel+Gale developed a bold, simple black-and-white solution that emphasizes the user benefits of the service

Teasing, but aspiring to the mainstream

Client	Kink (CyberNet Entertainment)
Brand story	An erotic website
Studio	MINE
Art director	Christopher Simmons
Designers	Tim Belonax and Christopher Simmons
Typeface	Hand-drawn
Color	Red (PMS 1797)
Design approach	This niche business hoped to enter the adult entertainment mainstream, and the "clean" logo refinement reflected this. The letter K is drawn to suggest wrought-iron implements, but in a friendly way, and the shield outline forms a corset, with its upper and lower contours delicately suggesting the curves of a woman's body. The cheerful red color, rather than being threatening, harks back to the efforts of the once-risqué Playboy brand to enter the mainstream

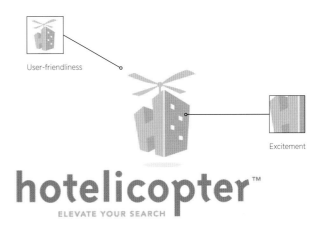

User-friendliness

Excitement

Client	Hotelicopter
Brand story	A web-search site that lets travelers find and book hotels at the lowest possible price
Studio	Stebler Creative
Designer	Jeremy Stebler
Typeface	Triplex Bold (modified)
Colors	Orange and gray (web/process colors)
Design approach	The website's new name contained the word "hotel," but combined it with an unexpected suffix to go with the tagline "Elevate your search." The designers felt that a literal illustration of the brand name, far from being trite, would work because of its unusual and fanciful nature. The result, which combines a rotor, a hotel, and the initial letter H, reinforces the name and helps to make it memorable. Its playful nature, typical of web designs, underscores the brand premise of being easy to grasp and fun to use

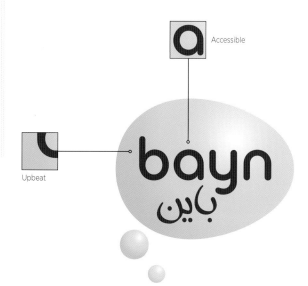

Accessible

Upbeat

Client	Bayn
Brand story	A prepaid, local-area network telephone service in Morocco, operated by Wana (formerly Maroc Connect)
Studio	Lippincott
Designer	Brendán Murphy
Strategy	Dennis Bonan and Kat Walker
Typeface	Bespoke
Colors	Deep blue (PMS 2738), green (PMS 376), and lime green (PMS 382)
Design approach	The service was designed to democratize access to telecommunications in Morocco and give some control back to consumers. The simple, rounded typography, set in a thought bubble rendered in bright green, signals a fresh approach, and clearly differentiates the brand from the more established operators it competes against. The flexibility to lead with either the Arabic or Latin alphabet for the Bayn name made it easier to adapt the identity to regional and national audiences

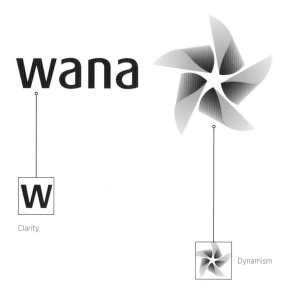

Clarity

Dynamism

Client	Wana
Brand story	A new telecommunications company in Morocco, offering fixed line, mobile, and Internet services. The core idea of the brand was to put the customer in control
Studio	Lippincott
Designers	Brendán Murphy and Julia McGreevy
Strategists	Dennis Bonan and Kat Walker
Typeface	Dax (redrawn)
Colors	Deep blue (PMS 2738), blue (PMS 2985), green (PMS 376), and lime green (PMS 382)
Design approach	Wana sought to make waves in the telecoms market in Morocco by delivering on its brand promise in everything from the name (which means "close to you"), to the identity design, the product experience, and the market offering. Every aspect of the brand design was carefully and deliberately crafted: the primary brand color—bright green—communicated a new idea and set the brand apart from the other phone companies. The symbol, a pinwheel star, evokes the star in the Moroccan flag and connects with the national spirit. The name, set in a friendly, lowercase font, sends a clear signal of easy accessibility

New horizon

Client	Neustar
Brand story	One of the firms responsible for Internet registry and connectivity
Studio	Siegel+Gale
Creative director	Young Kim
Design director	Lloyd Blander
Typeface	Bespoke
Colors	Green and yellow (process colors)
Design approach	The name is set in a simple Helvetica, with a gradation of lighter color slicing diagonally through the middle of it; the line cuts across the s and is continued through the angled ends of the u and t, tying together the two parts of the word. Without the assistance of an icon, this simple device evokes the new horizons of the Internet, the feeling of waking to a fresh start, turning a corner, or discovering a new solution to an old problem

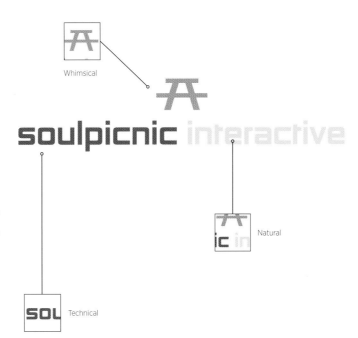

Whimsical

Natural

Technical

Client	Soulpicnic Interactive
Brand story	A web-development company
Studio	Think Studio, NYC
Designers	John Clifford and Herb Thornby
Typeface	Architype Ballmer
Colors	Brown (PMS 405) and green (PMS 372)
Design approach	As designer John Clifford explained, the challenge posed by the logo redesign for this web agency was that "it's a tech company, yet they wanted to show a more organic, friendly feel." The old logo had a hand-drawn, outdated look. Think Studio gave it a more professional appearance, while still reflecting the firm's personality and philosophy. The technical aspect is evident in the choice of type, but its hardness is offset by a natural palette of brown and green and the whimsy of a picnic table icon

137

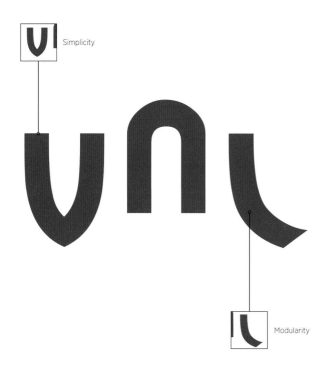

Simplicity

Modularity

Client VNL (Vihaan Networks Limited)

Brand story A telecommunications company, founded in India, making GSM equipment that is simple, modular, and easy to install, operate, and maintain. The equipment runs on sustainable energy sources such as solar or wind power, allowing operators to reach remote rural markets profitably

Studio Obos Creative

Designer Ethem Hürsu Öke

Typeface Handcrafted lettershapes

Color Blue (PMS 293)

Design approach The client wanted a logo that would reflect the company's adaptability, flexibility, modularity, and innovative technology. The designer was able to convey these abstract qualities visually by designing the letters V, N, and L using simple, slightly unorthodox arcs that suggest the elements of an innovative, modular system. The simple forms and color are easy to remember and reproduce for all manner of printed and digital media. In addition, the logo suggests an elephant, a rural workhorse in many parts of south Asia

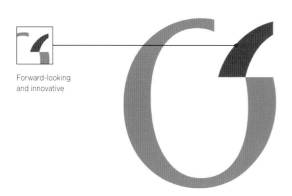

Forward-looking and innovative

Client Optima Telekom

Brand story A telecommunications company in Croatia

Studio Studio International

Designer Boris Ljubicic

Typefaces Aldine 721 BT and Verdana

Colors Red (PMS 1795) and grays (PMS 423 and and PMS 421)

Design approach The initial letter of the company name has a movable segment that is rotated to suggest a rotary phone dial or a telephone receiver. This reminds customers of the traditional market—domestic fixed lines—that make up much of Optima's business, and also suggests that the company has reoriented itself to provide other types of telephone service in the future

Client	Telephone.com (Xplorium Offshore)
Brand story	A web-based application providing telephony services, SMS text messaging, and other communication needs, targeting a young, tech-friendly crowd, but also wanting to appeal to less Internet-savvy users
Studio	PenguinCube
Designers	PenguinCube design team
Typeface	Dax (modified)
Color	Blue (PMS 295)
Design approach	The logo was inspired by the classic two cans connected by a long string. Another idea was to use "emoticons" made of punctuation marks to show different moods. Combining these ideas led to the open parentheses on either side of the name, allowing a variety of characters to occupy the space around the logo and communicate through it. As the business is web-based, it needed a logo that could be continually adapted, while the basic element remained constant, conveying reliability and remaining recognizable

Sober but adaptable

Client	CzechPoint
Brand story	An online e-government system that allows citizens of the Czech Republic to obtain information and public services easily via terminals in post offices and other locations
Studio	Lavmi
Designer	Babeta Ondrová
Typeface	DIN
Color	Light blue (PMS 2995)
Design approach	The idea behind an e-government system is that the data should do the running around rather than the person. CzechPoint uses modern technology to provide connectivity and contact so that citizens can track their paperwork and follow the course of their applications, cases, or requests, bringing greater transparency to most bureaucratic processes. In the bureaucracies of Prague and other Czech municipalities, this is a fairly revolutionary concept. The logo is formed from two spheres joining together, representing the government and its citizens. The sky-blue icon also resembles a pair of spyglasses, symbolizing the ability to see into the data system more clearly

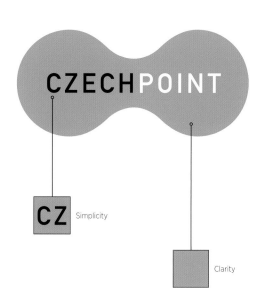

Simplicity

Clarity

GOTSPOT

Variations on a common theme give an identity versatility, interest, and an element of fun

Brand story Wireless Internet for cafés in the UK

Studio Fivefootsix

Typeface Avant Garde

Colors Red (PMS 186) and cyan (process color)

Design approach An ever-changing online digital world requires an ever-changing visual identity. The red central spot remains the same while the blue patterns emanating from it—radio waves, ripples, petals—change their patterns to remain interesting and engaging. The result is a bright, fun identity to capture and retain the imaginations of a young, web-savvy audience. The name provided a starting point and suggests continuous connectivity wherever the symbol can be seen. The symbol, in turn, is strong and memorable enough to work without the name, for example, on café windows.

The question arises, "Which version is the 'real' logo?" They all are. The beauty of this solution lies in the fact that the logo is the unifying concept, rather than a particular mark. There is no standard tie-in between the icons and the wordmark either; rather, it all works as part of a comprehensive identity system in which the designer works out the best way of applying the appropriate elements—icon, name, secondary graphics, typography—to the given context.

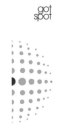

GOTSPOT LTD
WIRELESS INTERNET SOLUTIONS
90 WEST HILL
LONDON SW15 2UJ
T +44 (0)871 566 1416
F +44 (0)870 762 0351
WWW.GOTSPOT.CO.UK

DAVE BIRCH
DIRECTOR
M +44 (0)7966 439822
DAVE@GOTSPOT.CO.UK

The fronts of the business cards only show the name with the contact information; the backs have a cropped version of one of several alternate marks.

The alternate versions of the mark are connected by the central red dot, underscoring the brand concept that anyone can be connected to the Wi-Fi network.

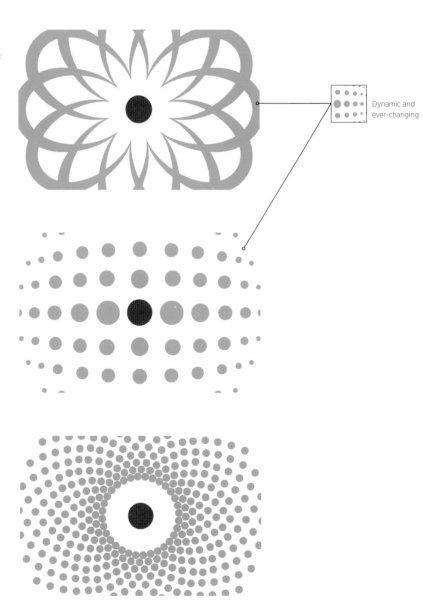

Dynamic and ever-changing

ARCHITECTURE & DESIGN

There's something about architects, graphic artists, and designers that makes them love the idea of having their own logo. Sometimes it's a matter of positioning their practice, or making a statement about the type of work they do; sometimes they're saying something about their own heritage or philosophical outlook; sometimes the logo illustrates their approach to the creative process, sometimes it's just a matter of personal whimsy. In the best cases, it can be all of the above.

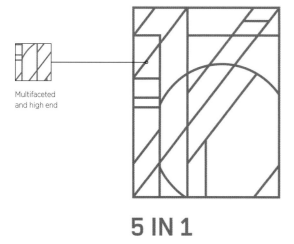

Multifaceted
and high end

5 IN 1

Client	Studio 5 in 1
Brand story	A multidisciplinary design collective working out of a retail storefront in Brooklyn, New York
Studio	//Avec
Designer	Camillia BenBassat
Designers/ Typographers	Joao Peres and Serhat Ferhat
Typeface	Foundry Monoline
Color	Gold (PMS 8660)
Design approach	The logo breaks down the numerals 1 and 5 to show how the various parts work together within, and for, the whole. The modernist style alludes to a number of artistic genres, with their connotations of quality and exclusivity. Members of this working collective come and go; each one can configure the logo to "self-brand" as part of the larger, shifting whole. The logo is used in-store where it works equally well in positive and negative versions. On business cards and stationery it is executed in gold foil on a variety of lush paper stocks that reinforce the richness of the multidisciplinary practice

Client	Black Hare Studio
Brand story	A letterpress and fine-art studio in Texas, USA
Designer	Virginia Green
Typefaces	Janson and Myriad Pro-Light
Colors	Beige (PMS 9080), red (PMS 193), and black
Design approach	The designer's objective was to come up with an identity that reflects the art studio's combination of traditional and modern creative techniques. The audience is clients looking for unique ways of solving their visual problems; the designer's challenge was to convey a variety of printing methods in one icon. Her inspiration was Black Hare Studio's fondness for rabbits—both their physical characteristics and what they symbolize in human society. According to the designer, "the grace and elegance of the animal's posture combined with a graphic sensibility" to reflect the client's personal style and provide an icon for the studio brand

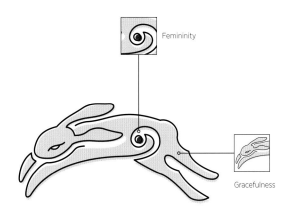

Femininity

Gracefulness

Client	No. Twelve Queen Street
Brand story	A small interior design consultancy in Bath, UK
Agency	Irving & Co.
Designer	Julian Roberts
Typographer	Peter Horridge
Typeface	Hand-lettered calligraphy
Color	Green (PMS 384)
Design approach	The firm wanted a new identity that would reflect Bath's Georgian heritage, but reinterpret it with a modern, highly crafted design approach. The penmanship of George Bickham provided the inspiration for this fancy wordmark, which reflects the company's high standards, and positions the brand at the top of its profession

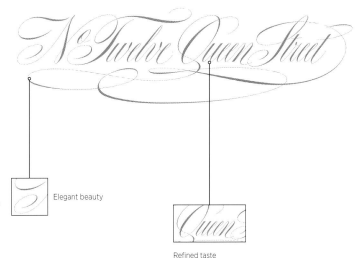

Elegant beauty

Refined taste

Tactile

Economical

Client Rui Grazina—Arquitectura+Design

Brand story Portuguese architecture firm looking for a clean, professional identity to reflect the two sides of its business

Studio Playout

Designer Tiago Machado

Typeface Cargo Bold

Colors Brown and gray

Design approach The aim was to portray the fields of architecture and design, without revealing a bias toward any particular style. The challenge was to create an identity that could be used to sign pieces inexpensively (the logo can be used as a stencil). The two-texture solution links the activities of architecture (concrete) and design (wood)

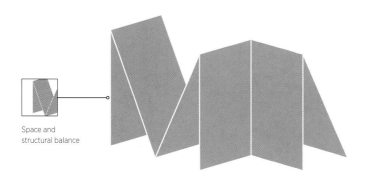

Space and structural balance

Client Studio Ma / Architecture and Environmental Design

Brand story A collaborative, design-focused architecture firm in Phoenix, Arizona, USA, that aims to create beautiful spaces supported by accessible, functional, and conscientious forms

Studio //Avec

Designers Camillia BenBassat and Evan Dody

Typeface Bespoke

Color Gray (PMS Cool Gray 8)

Design approach The designers wanted to avoid a typical architect's word-type logo, so they looked to the "space as substance" philosophy of the architects' methodology for inspiration, and combined this with the attributes of balance and dimension. The spaces within and between the letters remind one of the functional architectural spaces in a building. The designers also wanted a mark that could stand alone, without the support of the words. The logo captures the values of the Studio Ma practice and provides a basis for communication that allows it to continue evolving conceptually and visually

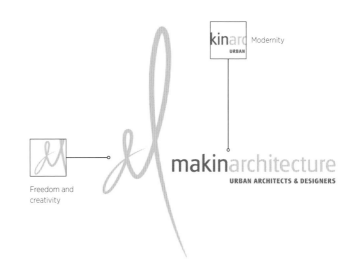

Modernity

Freedom and
creativity

Client Makin Architecture

Brand story Architects and urban designers needed
a new name and logo after one of the
partners retired

Studio Imagine-cga

Designer David Caunce

Typeface Glasgow

Colors Orange (PMS 130) and gray (PMS 431)

**Design
approach** The sweeping, free-form initial M reflects
the creative thought processes that
go into the firm's projects. The change
from the previous identity also indicated
a repositioning of Makin as a contemporary,
forward-thinking practice

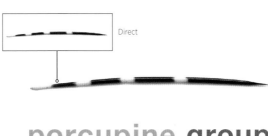

Direct

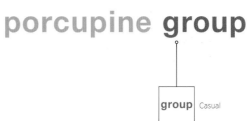

Casual

Client Porcupine Group

Brand story An interior design firm in New York City
with a philosophy that is simple and
direct, without ornamentation, using bold
touches of color in its work

Studio Think Studio, NYC

Designers John Clifford and Herb Thornby

Typeface Helvetica Neue Bold

Colors Orange (PMS 151) and gray (PMS 431)

**Design
approach** The firm shies away from using ornamental
or decorative solutions, so the logo
needed to reflect that. The firm got its
name from the owner's admiring the
beauty of porcupine quills. At first the
designers explored ways of incorporating
quills in a more abstract manner, but in the
end decided that a photograph of a single
quill was the most effective visual solution.
The lowercase typography reflects the
friendly, casual atmosphere of the firm.
Overall, the simplicity and directness of
the logo help the firm stand out from the
more decorative looks adopted by many
interior design firms

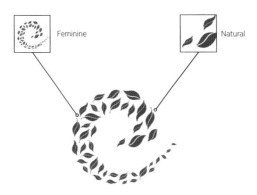

Feminine

Natural

environmental construction, inc.

unique and inspired landscape designs

Client Environmental Construction, Inc. (ECI)

Brand story A "green" landscaping company in the USA that focuses on craft and design

Studio McBreen Design, Inc.

Designer Craig McBreen

Typefaces Folio Medium Condensed and Light Condensed

Color Green (PMS 364)

Design approach In addition to updating the logo to better represent the company's environmentally sensitive approach and attention to the craft of landscape design, the designer sought to create a mark that would have explicit appeal to women, who are a very important part of the audience for this business. The mark is as effective standing alone as it is with the name and tagline

KATHERINE ANDERSON

LANDSCAPE ARCHITECTURE

Spare and modernist

Chic

Client Katherine Anderson Landscape Architecture

Brand story A landscape architect with a pared-down, modernist aesthetic

Studio Mary Hutchison Design

Designer Mary Chin Hutchison

Typeface Helvetica Light

Colors Green (PMS 390) and gray (PMS 491)

Design approach The mark plays with the negative spaces of Katherine Anderson's initials (which have no curves, only straight lines), to form an abstract visual reference to paving stones and lawn areas. The logo is modernist and minimal, but the colors keep it grounded in the traditional materials of landscape architecture

Client	Green Town
Brand story	A Ukrainian company working in both building and landscape design
Studio	Korolivski Mitci
Art director	Viktoriia Korol
Designer	Dmytro Korol
Typeface	[None]
Colors	Green (PMS 361) and orange (PMS 021)
Design approach	The immediately recognizable symbols of a peaked roof with a little chimney to denote building and a leaf to denote gardening are combined in a clean, original way to create a pleasing new icon that conveys the integration of these two disciplines. The complementary colors are necessary to make it work: in black-and-white, the point would be lost

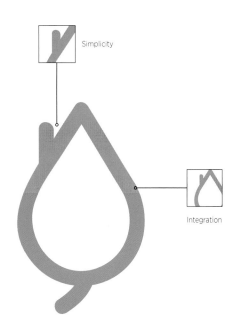

Simplicity

Integration

Client	Flowers of the World
Brand story	An upmarket florist in New York that combines scientific knowledge of flowers with artistic craft arrangements to create bouquets that are both beautiful and intriguing
Studio	Inaria
Creative director	Andrew Thomas
Designers	Andrew Thomas, Ange Luke, and Lynne Devine
Typeface	Gill Sans
Colors	Black with silver gloss foil
Design approach	This simple, precise logo conveys both the scientific and artistic aspects of the florist's work: the lines build up to give the impression of a flower's petals in the same way a bouquet is built into a beautiful creation through the careful addition of layers of blossoms

Elegant and sophisticated

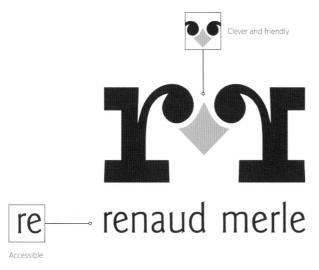

Clever and friendly

Accessible

Client	Renaud Merle
Brand story	A French graphic designer specializing in identity graphics
Designer	Renaud Merle
Typeface	Goudy Sans
Colors	Yellow (PMS 130) and gray (PMS Cool Gray 11)
Design approach	"Merle" is French for blackbird and the duplicated r not only forms a letter M, but with the simple addition of a yellow diamond, it also makes a playful drawing of a bird's head. The clean, spare forms belie a playful identity that uses literary and visual puns to convey the intelligence and creativity of this designer

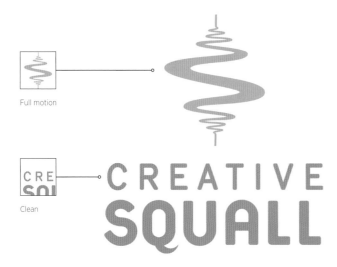

Full motion

Clean

Client	Creative Squall
Brand story	An independent design studio, based in Texas, USA, providing naming and design of logos and brand collateral materials
Studio	Creative Squall
Designer	Tad Dobbs
Typefaces	District Thin (modified) and Base 9 B (modified)
Colors	Orange (PMS 151) and gray (PMS Warm Gray 9)
Design approach	The designer aimed to capture the power and energy of his creative process (which is also suggested by the name of the company, a "squall" being both a war cry and a sudden storm) in a way that would also convey the clean, spare style of many of his designs. The orange and gray refer to the pencils he has used for years to sketch out ideas. "The pencils aren't that great, but I came to realize that the colors, specifically the orange, appeal to me," says Tad Dobbs. Although his initial sketches are very quick and loose, the finished work is typically "very clean and simple, much like the finished mark"

Client	Korolivski Mitci
Brand story	A Ukrainian design studio whose work accentuates national design traditions
Studio	Korolivski Mitci
Art director	Dmytro Korol
Designer	Viktoriia Korol
Typeface	Bespoke, based on traditional Cyrillic handlettering
Colors	Red (PMS 485) and black
Design approach	The surname of the designers is Korol, which means "King"; Korolivski Mitci means "the King's artists." Much of their work is for Ukrainian companies and they pride themselves in drawing on the rich visual heritage of their country. The colors, patterns, and old-fashioned lettering of their logo are redolent of Ukrainian folk designs used to decorate clothing and painted eggs, while the stark forms and bold pencil shape (together with their slick website) make it clear that their work is entirely up-to-date

КОРОЛІВСЬКІ МИТЦІ

Simultaneously traditional and modern

Client	Natoof Design
Brand story	A small design studio in Dubai providing design services for both personal and corporate clients, especially young business leaders and entrepreneurs starting up or relaunching their brands
Studio	Natoof Design
Designer	Mariam bin Natoof
Typeface	Bespoke
Color	Black
Design approach	The family name of the agency's founder is short and easy to pronounce and remember, so it made sense to use it as a central feature of the visual identity. Using the name this way communicates a feeling of uniqueness and approachability, setting the agency apart from the large, multinational design and advertising agencies against which Natoof competes. The blending of Arabic calligraphy and English typeface shows that Natoof is comfortable integrating the two cultures

natoof

Original and approachable

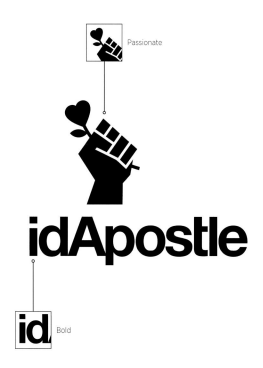

Passionate

Bold

idApostle

Client	idApostle
Brand story	An identity designer and consultant based in Ottawa, Canada
Studio	idApostle
Designer	Steve Zelle
Typeface	Helvetica Neue Bold
Color	Black
Design approach	The aim was to capture the design firm's passion and experience. As the designer explains, "We wanted to balance our qualities of love and strength in a clean and bold manner." The company's tagline is "An identity love affair." The resulting symbol conveys a positive attitude and implies a productive relationship with clients, many of whom are start-ups with a similarly bold attitude

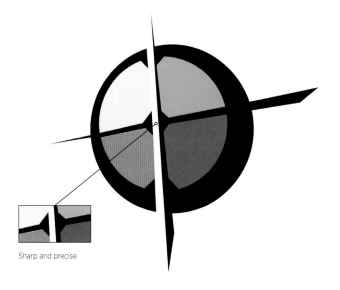

Sharp and precise

Client	Erik Borreson Design
Brand story	A graphic designer in Wisconsin, USA, working mostly on print projects
Studio	Erik Borreson Design
Designer	Erik Borreson
Typeface	Bespoke
Colors	Cyan, magenta, yellow, and black (process colors)
Design approach	The designer wanted a logo that would communicate the fact that his projects are almost exclusively in the field of print. He also required a mark that would have some shelf life. He sought inspiration in a variety of symbols relating to the idea of print before settling on a combination of his initials, EB, and the registration marks used to align the printing plates in four-color (CMYK) printing

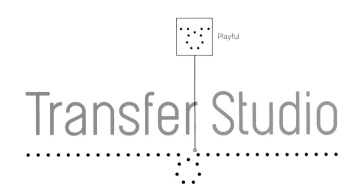

Playful

Client — Transfer Studio

Brand story — A design studio in London that produces work for print, exhibitions, and events

Studio — Transfer Studio

Designers — Valeria Hedman and Falko Grentrup

Typeface — Konrad

Color — Blue (PMS 132)

Design approach — After establishing themselves with a reputation for "imaginative and thoughtful design," the designers needed an identity that would help them progress. They wanted something that would focus on their solutions-oriented approach with a simple and straightforward design system. The font's friendly curves and open letters make the approachable character of the designers clear and reinforce the playful nature of their work. The logo is applied to a wide range of materials, reflecting the designers' passion for print and setting an example for clients to follow

Client — Vivio World, Inc.

Brand story — A creative team in Poland inventing new experiences for mobile platforms and social websites

Studio — Insane Facilities

Designer — Jarek Berecki

Typeface — Bespoke

Color — Magenta (process color)

Design approach — The studio needed a logo that captured both its creative style and the focus of its work, which is mastering the user experience and communication-oriented applications. The speech bubble forms the basis of the symbol and a cheerful, animated font conveys an impression of activity. The resulting impression is one of positivity and creativity

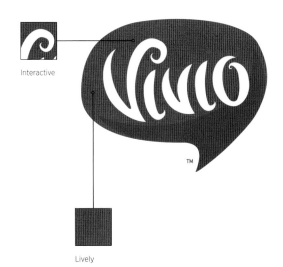

Interactive

Lively

151

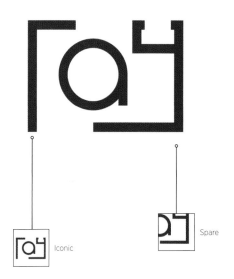

Client   Ray Watkins

Brand story   A commercial photographer who has worked with some big-name subjects in the UK, including Lewis Hamilton and David Beckham

Studio   Pencil

Designer   Luke Manning

Typeface   Bespoke

Color   Dark gray (PMS 447)

Design approach   The design agency wanted to give the photographer an identity that focused on the primary tool of his trade. Camera bodies are covered with lots of little icons, indicating all their settings and functions. Using the three letters of Ray's name, the designer crafted an iconic symbol of a classic SLR camera, exhibiting confidence and competence within the field of commercial photography

Iconic

Spare

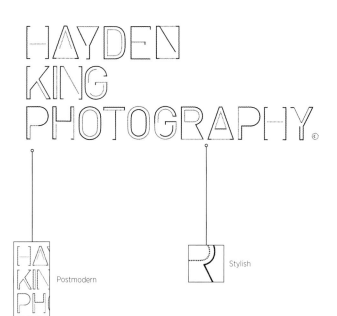

Client   Hayden King Photography

Brand story   A fashion and studio photography agency

Studio   Frank & Proper

Designer   Brett King

Typeface   Bespoke, based on DIN; every letter is different

Colors   Black and white

Design approach   The logo consists of a specially crafted, stylized font inspired by the little holes on a roll of film and the rapid clicking of a camera shutter. It captures the notion of fashion and style without resorting to clichés of photographic symbolism or imagery. Each letter is different, just as every photograph is a unique capture of a subject and a moment. Although the letterforms are simple, like well-crafted photographic images, they invite the eye to linger and explore

Postmodern

Stylish

Client	Barry White
Brand story	An established fine artist who accepts corporate and personal commissions, as well as exhibiting in galleries
Studio	Imagine-cga
Designer	David Caunce
Typefaces	Bespoke, based on Barry White's signature, with Humanist 777
Colors	Black and white
Design approach	"There was, of course, another Barry White," writes the designer David Caunce, referring to the famous singer. "We chose to use the 'White' part of Barry's signature to avoid any confusion." The resulting logo frames the brushstroke, which conveys the natural media in which the artist works, in a contrasting square. Clean type spells out his name and adds the words "Fine Artist" to make things perfectly clear. In a sense, Mr. White's signature has been his logo since he started painting. Using that as the basis for his brand captures the one-off nature of his work, and establishes his professional credentials in the context of his art busines

Personal

Barry White · Individual

Client	Kool Kat Jackson's
Brand story	Business run by a Los Angeles–based artist
Studio	Andy Gabbert Design
Designer	Andy Gabbert
Typeface	Hand-drawn
Colors	Blue (PMS 544), green (PMS 375), and black
Design approach	To echo the artist's own "antic art," the logo was hand-drawn to be energetic and enjoyable. Its influences are the same as the artist's: classic cars; pinups; nostalgic imagery from 1950s California, including classic signs from the Los Angeles area; and album-cover art from the era of rockabilly, swing, and blues. The aim was to strike a balance between retaining a spontaneous, quality and appearing too refined

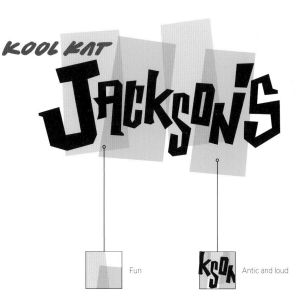

Fun

Antic and loud

ELEMENTAL

A minimalist design approach works well, if it is appropriate to the brand philosophy

Brand story A New York–based architecture firm, founded in 2006, whose philosophy and practice are based on principles of environmental sustainability

Studio //Avec

Designer Camillia BenBassat

Typeface Helvetica Neue

Color Black

Design approach Although a young firm, Elemental builds on the experience of its principals, who have more than 50 years of individual practice between them, continuing a design tradition directly inherited from the early modernists. To reflect this heritage and commitment to the ideals of modernism, the designers developed a name and identity that incorporate archetypal components informed by a minimalist aesthetic: the golden ratio, monochromatic presentation, and the Helvetica typeface.

The logo—a lowercase name set in a font that epitomizes modernist sensibilities—could not be more functionalist. And yet this simplicity, like that of modern architecture itself, is deceptive. The type has been carefully spaced, and the way the logo is incorporated into the design of items such as business cards, letterhead, website, and brochures, is deliberately considered. Layouts are based on the golden ratio—the proportion at the heart of the golden rectangle, the classical spiral, and the Fibonacci series. This spatial relationship occurs throughout nature and the history of architecture; such a reference to nature and cultural patrimony supports the Elemental brand concept and values.

As though trying to push the simple, type-only logo even further into the realm of minimalist aesthetic, some of the agency's materials use a black-on-black blind debossing technique.

elemental

 Simplicity and modernity

To underscore the functionalist brand identity, brochures are printed in black and white, with a typographic treatment that reiterates the aesthetic direction established by the logo.

CORPORATE

The "corporate" logo is often a metaphor for a heavyweight symbol representing an entity that's impersonal and unapproachable, with conservative values that defy humanity and command respect. But today the reality is usually different. The following examples show that even the largest corporation, carrying on the most serious business, can express a warm, friendly personality that appeals to our emotions and sense of individuality.

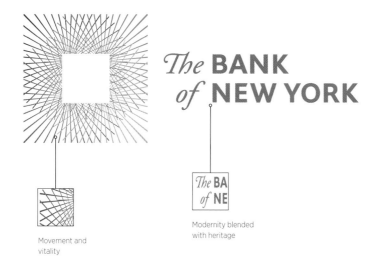

Movement and vitality

Modernity blended with heritage

Client	The Bank of New York
Brand story	Founded in 1784, the bank is the oldest in the USA. In the mid-1990s it began a period of aggressive acquisition that turned it into a financial powerhouse
Studio	Lippincott
Art director	Connie Birdsall
Designers	Alex de Jánosi, Ryan Kovalak, and Jenifer Lehker
Strategy	Suzanne Hogan
Typefaces	Bliss and Garamond (redrawn)
Colors	Blue-gray (PMS 431) with orange (PMS 144), blue (PMS 300), green (PMS 355), and orange-red (PMS 485)
Design	The graphic element of this logo was inspired by the intricate patterns of currencies, stocks, and bonds, with four distinct sets of radiating lines and overlapping colors used to signify an array of financial offerings and the bank's collaborative relationships with clients. The interwoven lines suggest movement and the vitality of financial markets. The white square symbolizes the expertise in each of the bank's core businesses. The type for the wordmark combines a traditional serif typeface with a modern, sans serif, suggesting the modernization of an established entity and emphasizing the core elements of the name

© Andy Shen

© Jeffrey Totaro

Client	Mark Snow
Brand story	A holistic business consultant based in the UK
Agency	Planet
Designer	Bobbie Haslett
Typeface	Helvetica Neue Bold
Color	Purple (PMS 249)
Design approach	The consultant works with both companies and individuals, helping them develop their personal strengths to achieve natural growth in their business. The identity needed to convey this, while feeling friendly and not forced. The designer explored the idea of a chestnut coming out of its shell to make a symbol that is friendly and approachable; the lowercase typography reinforces these values, while the deep purple suggests a passion for helping others. Mark Snow's competitors generally use more corporate-looking logos, so this solution differentiates his brand effectively

Organic

mark snow
holistic consultant

Sense of passion and commitment

Client	Hays
Brand story	A worldwide recruitment and human resources consultancy
Studio	Interbrand
Art director	Paul Smith
Typeface	Bespoke
Colors	Blues (process colors)
Design approach	To reflect the many areas of expert recruitment in which Hays is involved, the designers decided to use a bold H and populate the shape of the letter with a broad variety of textures and patterns symbolizing different industries and professions. The icon is often applied in large-scale displays at airports and trade fairs, where it can be complemented by different text claims. The many textures give the identity visual interest, breadth, and variety, yet are united by form and color. As blue is a key component of many corporate brand identities (signifying dependability and reliability), and human resources is an area in which trust and confidence are important, this color serves as a reassurance to clients and a reminder of Hays' sensitivity to their concerns

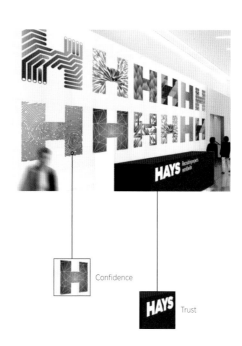

Confidence

Trust

Forward momentum

Health

Client	Pfizer
Brand story	A global pharmaceutical giant seeking a subtle update to its 1991 blue oval logo that would retain existing brand equity, but reflect two decades of changes, including expansion into new areas
Studio	Siegel+Gale
Creative directors	Sven Seger and Young Kim
Design director	Johnny Lim
Designers	Monica Chai, Quae Luong, and Dave McCanless
Typeface	Bespoke
Color	Blue (process blend)
Design approach	The oval logo had positive customer associations worldwide, but Pfizer has changed since that logo was adopted, developing life-changing new medicines. By tilting the oval, brightening the color, and modifying the typeface to make it more approachable, Siegel+Gale preserves its equity, but offers "a fresh look at Pfizer." The new identity communicates the company's vision of better health care around the world

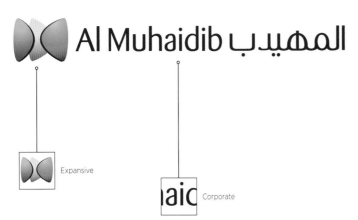

Expansive

Corporate

Client	Al Muhaidib
Brand story	A Saudi conglomerate with global interests in industrial goods and services, energy, retail, finance, and real estate
Studio	Fitch
Art director/ Designer	Anis Bengiuma
Typeface	Barmeno
Colors	Deep blue type, with green, yellow-orange, and light blue for the mark
Design approach	Al Muhaidib's activities have such a broad reach, finding a symbol to reflect that was the main challenge. The identity had to look international, while resonating with a Saudi audience. The client's global reach was the designer's inspiration. He took the "orange-peel" outline of a world map as a basic symbol and used over-lapping areas of color to denote the company's diversity and activities in multiple sectors. Combined with a modern, but austere type solution in a classic deep blue, the result is a logo that is memorable, stands out from the competition, and reflects the values of unity, diversity, and entrepreneurship

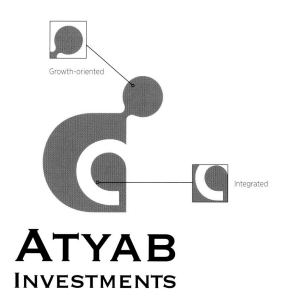

Growth-oriented

Integrated

Client Atyab Investments

Brand story An investment firm, based in the Gulf nation of Oman, seeking to diversify from its origins in the food industry

Studio Paragon Marketing Communications

Designer Konstantin Assenov

Typeface Copperplate (modified)

Colors Bronze (process color) and black

Design approach Starting with an abstract lowercase a, the designer crafted a form that conveys the idea of "input leading to output," with the smaller circle at upper right rising out of the a like a sun ascending or a loaf of bread rising (the firm began as an arm of Oman Flour Mills), suggesting profit or return on investment. The simple form combined with a deep, warm color suggests health and integration

ATYAB
INVESTMENTS

Ascendant

Corporate

Client Qipco Holding

Brand story A holding company based in Doha, Qatar, that has diversified its interests in real estate, construction, oil and gas, trading, and finance, to include health and joint ventures. Rapidly becoming a global player, it needed a world-class identity

Studio Fitch

Art director/ Designer Anis Bengiuma

Typeface Gotham

Colors Dark blue (PMS 295) and cyan (process color)

Design approach Qipco needed to align its core values and visual language. The starburst mark hints at a sun as well as a globe, denoting its aspirations as well as its current activities. The name, spelled out in capital letters, reinforces this with its repeating round forms evoking solidity. Taking one of the star's rays as the tail of the Q integrates the two parts of the logo and conveys the idea that all the global activities benefit the base. By positioning Qipco among the leading global players, the new identity enables it to become even more diversified in the future

Bright

Not intimidating

Client Cash Plus Credit Services

Brand story An online service based in the US state of Maryland that offers short-term loans, typically to lower- and middle-income customers in their mid-20s to early 40s. The fastest-growing segment of the company's market is Hispanic customers

Studio Mosaic Creative LLC

Art director/ Designer Tad Dobbs

Typefaces Interstate Regular (modified) and Eidetic Neo

Colors Blue (PMS 307) and green (PMS 376)

Design approach The designer and client wanted a friendly, vibrant, and inviting identity. A fresh and energetic color palette, supported by the up-to-date feel of the sans-serif type, makes the brand appear accessible and fun. The resulting look differentiates the company from more typically conservative financial institutions that use a darker palette to indicate the idea of money. The plus sign embedded in the name puts the positive feelings at the heart of the logo, suggesting a cheerful, worry-free brand

Optimistic

Forward thinking

Client Neuroad Ventures

Brand story A joint venture capital firm investing in Internet start-ups

Studio Insane Facilities

Designer Jarek Berecki

Typeface Bespoke

Colors Multicolored

Design approach The name is a play on "neuro," as in networked cells, and "road," as in the information superhighway. The designer wanted a handcrafted look and, inspired by a human neuron cell, opted for the organic curves and colorful blends that would suggest the rapidly firing synapses of an intelligent organization. The colorful logo (reminiscent of the rainbow-striped Apple logo used in the 1980s) also looks good on a white background. Its modern, happy feeling is augmented by a somewhat unorthodox font from a small type foundry

Client Daiwa House Group

Brand story Japan's second-largest house builder

Studio Interbrand

Typeface Bespoke

Colors Red (process blends) and black

Design approach Despite being one of Japan's top house builders, Daiwa faced some future uncertainty with Japan's low birthrate and a rapidly aging society. Interbrand's research showed that to meet its goals, the company would have to improve its image among employees and with the general public. The revised brand strategy included better communication with customers, so Interbrand designed a new brand identity to convey the renewed focus on human interaction. The logo is based on a red circle, a very traditional Japanese sign, turned into a heart-shaped band that symbolizes the life cycle, nesting, and security

Domestic stability

Japanese

Daiwa House ®
Group

Client International Islamic Trade Finance Corporation (ITFC)

Brand story An organization established to help businesses in Muslim countries obtain better access to trade finance and the know-how to compete globally, building stronger trade links and improving the livelihoods of individuals

Studio Siegel+Gale

Typeface Officina Sans

Colors Palette of 12 colors, from amber to stone to sand

Design approach Crafted from 12 interlocking arrows that radiate from the center, the colorful logo reflects the values of human partnership, interconnection, and technical prowess. The heart of the logo alludes strongly to traditional Islamic art and culture, while the palette reinforces the regional focus of the brand. The name is set in a modern, sans-serif lowercase, which conveys the values of humanity and clarity that define ITFC's approach to business, both with financing partners and with their end customers. The initials are a deep red, communicating passion, energy, and drive

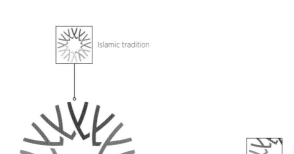

Islamic tradition

Open

itfc
International
Islamic Trade
Finance Corporation

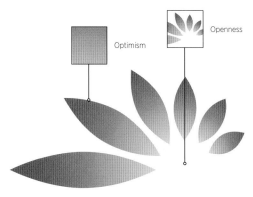

Optimism

Openness

Client	Mashreq Bank
Brand story	A banking and financial services firm based in the United Arab Emirates
Studio	Lippincott
Art director	Alex de Janosi
Designers	Jenifer Lehker and Sam Ayling
Typeface	Corisande (redrawn)
Colors	Deep blue (PMS 2738) and yellow (PMS 109) shading to red (PMS 1788)
Design approach	Mashreq, Arabic for bright, is also the name given to the lands east of Cairo. The logo was inspired by the metaphor of a rising sun or an opening flower, and the symbol suggests the opening up of possibilities: financial opportunities, access to service, human relationships

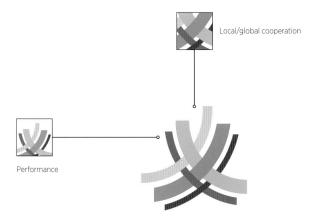

Local/global cooperation

Performance

Client	First Citizens Bank
Brand story	A global financial services firm based in Trinidad and Tobago
Studio	Lippincott
Art director	Connie Birdsall
Designers	Julia McGreevy, Ippolita Ferrari, and Kevin Hammond
Strategy	James Bell
Typeface	Bliss (redrawn)
Colors	Bottle green (PMS 347), emerald green (PMS 368), orange-red (PMS 485), yellow (PMS 123), and blue (PMS 285)
Design approach	As the bank sought to expand its services, a fresh identity gave it the basis from which to renew its communications in the local market and establish its international credibility at the same time. The interlocking arches, thrusting upward, suggest energy and growth, symbolizing partnership and cooperation. The colors represent the vibrant, multicultural Caribbean, as well as the diversity of global markets. Green is still predominant, to build on the brand's existing recognition. The title-case name, set in a friendly, sans-serif font, reminds audiences of the bank's flexibility and commitment to customers

Partnership and connectivity

Client Arctaris Capital Partners

Brand story A firm providing capital investment to public and private companies

Studio TippingSprung

Designer Paul Gardner

Typeface ATSackers

Colors Light green (PMS 376) and dark green (PMS 348)

Design approach The firm specializes in providing capital infusions just when their clients have reached a turning point and are ready for expansion. Turning the letter C into the shape of a puzzle piece conveys the idea that the connection of money and opportunity is not automatic, but requires skillful and creative placement, which underlines the brand idea of providing a niche service in the market

ARCTARIS

Financial growth

Stability

Client China Merchants Securities

Brand story Founded in 1991, this subsidiary of the century-old China Merchants Group is now one of China's top 10 firms in securities investment and financial services

Studio Interbrand China

Art director Chuan Jiang

Designers Chuan Jiang and Miao Jie Li

Typeface Hand-drawn

Colors Red and gold icon with black pictographs

Design approach The old logo didn't fully reflect the brand's aspirations of rigor and integrity, or its strategic strengths of innovation, a broad range of offerings, and a long-term commitment to the market. The new logo keeps the circular C wrapped around an M made up of three 1's, to imply leadership, and adds an upturned underline, suggesting a confident smile; the three 1's and the underline also form the Chinese character for mountain, reinforcing the sense of stability and long-term wealth appreciation, and also job security for employees. The 3D effect makes the new logo dynamic and contemporary, while the metallic texture alludes to traditional Chinese bronze and china work, both long symbols of wealth

招商证券
China Merchants Securities

Confidence

Simple and clean

Risk Management Planning, LLC

Client	Risk Management Planning
Brand story	A service to identify risk and develop a plan to minimize said risk
Studio	Clay McIntosh Creative
Designer	Clay McIntosh
Typefaces	Fenice, with name in Trade Condensed
Colors	Red (PMS 186), gray (PMS 428), and black
Design approach	The red lowercase r hiding within the big black m provides a clear and immediate illustration of the service provided—isolating the "risk" within the "management" is what the company does. It is not often that letterforms lend themselves so well to this kind of play. In this case, the designer has taken full advantage of a bit of visual cleverness that is natural and unforced; humorous but, thanks to its crisp rendering, entirely appropriate to a serious business

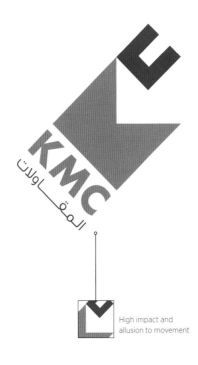

High impact and
allusion to movement

Client	KMC
Brand story	The real-estate management division of Asyad, a large Kuwait-based construction firm. KMC engages in project management and other consultancy work
Studio	Fitch
Designer	Steve Burden
Typefaces	Bespoke, with Futura
Colors	Orange (PMS 1665) and indigo (PMS 302)
Design approach	Fitch was hired to come up with a new brand identity just as the company was being redefined. The letters KMC provided a starting point for the designer, who then abstracted them into an arrangement of geometric forms that plays with figure and ground (the M is found in the negative space between the K and C) and creates a sense of motion. The result is legible and has a memorable impact, successfully replacing the complicated previous identity

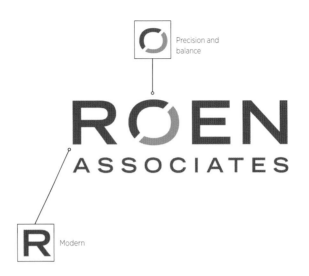

Precision and balance

Modern

Client Røen Associates

Brand story Founded in 1988 by Roger Røen, the firm is involved in several areas relating to construction management, providing architects with services including cost estimations, project management, and viability studies of construction projects

Studio Mary Hutchison Design

Designer Mary Chin Hutchison

Typeface Trade Gothic LH Bold Extended

Colors Dark blue (PMS 541) and light blue (PMS 542)

Design approach The old logo was poorly crafted, with no equity to salvage for the new identity created on this firm's twentieth anniversary. The new font is modern and well balanced, customized to take advantage of a quirk in the orthography—the slash through the o—to represent the balance between cost-engineering and design, while also hinting at the top of a screw, an essential ingredient in construction

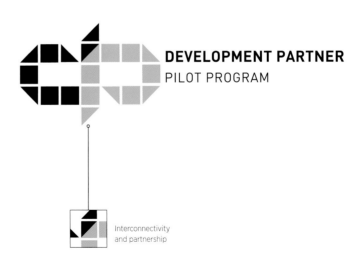

Interconnectivity and partnership

Client Development Partner Pilot Program

Brand story A pilot program set up to interact with the business alliances of the Grace Construction Company

Studio Alternative Production/Juno Studio

Designer Jun Li

Typeface Bespoke

Colors Green (Pantone DS 295-1), blue (Pantone DS 221-5), and brown (Pantone DS 13-3)

Design approach The logo is based on the concept of building blocks, with the d and p interlocking to reinforce the idea of partnership. In the early stages of design, the designer and client experimented with using blue or brown to bring in some of the values associated with those colors (blue: uplifting and powerful; brown: the character of building materials). In the end, they decided to underscore the relationship to the parent company by using the green of the Grace identity

BRISTLECONE ADVISORS

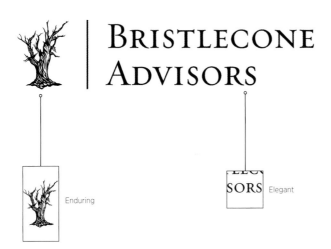

Enduring

SORS Elegant

Client	Bristlecone Advisors
Brand story	A western US financial planning firm wishing to project the image of a trusted, secure, enduring firm providing personal service
Studio	Mary Hutchison Design
Designer	Mary Chin Hutchison
Typeface	Requiem Text HTF Roman (adjusted to balance capitals)
Colors	Black and burgundy (PMS 7421)
Design approach	On their first meeting, the firm informed the designer that they did not seek a radical departure from their previous logo, which included an image of a bristlecone pine, one of the world's oldest trees, and a dated-looking font. To preserve as much equity as possible from the original logo and reassure clients of the security, trustworthiness, and endurance of the brand, the concept of a tree was retained, as were the colors. The tree was redrawn in a more timeless style and the font was updated with a more elegant, classic choice

BUSINESS CONTINUITY MANAGEMENT

 Dependable

 Reassuring

Client	Business Continuity Management (BCM) (Barclays Global Investors)
Brand story	A program designed to ensure that Barclays Global Investors' key businesses can continue to function in the event of a disaster or other threat
Studio	Andy Gabbert Design
Project manager	Ann Hirsch
Designer	Andy Gabbert
Typeface	Expert Sans Extra Bold
Color	Green (PMS 368)
Design approach	The program has to meet regulatory requirements and sustain client and shareholder confidence in the face of unpredictable circumstances. The designer commented, "Working with everything from crisis management to natural disasters and safety threats, visualizing BCM could itself have been a catastrophe. Focusing on the positive, I decided to accent their main function—continuity." The program is managed in partnership with numerous operating teams, such as facilities management and IT. One early idea for the logo involved an electric plug being reconnected. This evolved into the connected Ns of the final logo

Client	Large Left Brain LLC
Brand story	An IT firm providing support for the insurance industry
Studio	Mary Hutchison Design
Designer	Mary Chin Hutchison
Typeface	Adobe Garamond
Colors	Blue (PMS 654) and green (PMS 384)
Design approach	This start-up firm needed a polished corporate identity that conveyed its technical expertise as well as its all-encompassing approach to IT solutions. The infinity symbol conveys the idea of being part of a continuous system, while the specific way in which it is rendered, with two colors twisted into a 3D form, indicates that the firm is a dynamic problem solver that frees up its clients to focus on right-brain activities

Dynamic continuity

Client	Starr Tincup
Brand story	A Texas firm providing marketing services to the "human capital" industry, which includes recruitment and human resources
Studio	Starr Tincup
Designer	Tad Dobbs
Typeface	Gothic 13 (modified)
Colors	Red (PMS Red 032) and black
Design approach	The brand had a youthful, rebellious personality, but needed to project a more professional and experienced image to its audience of marketing managers, VPs, and CEOs at human resources firms. The pinching of the outline form alludes to comic-book art, while the overall design is inspired by classic workmen's shirts, sports logos, and other Western imagery in honor of the firm's pride in its roots in Fort Worth, Texas, USA. The logo takes on different personalities through the use of a different color palette and background textures in different applications. The result maintains the old attitude, but gives it a much more professional look

Modern Western

Fresh attitude

PAUL WU & ASSOCIATES

Clever visual humor can be appropriate to business services, and also builds an emotional bond with the brand

Brand story An accounting firm in Vancouver, Canada, whose local clientele is often Asian. The firm wanted to emphasize its specialized services, personal attention, and long-term stability

Studio Nancy Wu Design

Designer Nancy Wu

Typeface Neuzeit S

Colors Black (silver on collateral materials) and red (PMS 207)

Design approach The conceptual approach was to develop a well-crafted symbol that would be easily understood by speakers of any language. The client and designer wanted to avoid relying on English words or idioms, or falling back on financial clichés or overly abstract thinking that didn't accurately reflect the firm's grounded approach and honesty. Paul Wu's team sought to present themselves as smart, experienced thinkers with a strong, honest work ethic. The visual identity needed to relate these concepts in a modern, approachable manner.

The result reflects Paul Wu's thoughtful personality as a creative accountant with vision and balanced thinking, punctuated with the confident smile that comes from having satisfied customers. Paul Wu himself wears glasses, has an easygoing demeanor and smile, and is confident in his knowledge, experience, honest work ethic, and high standards of professionalism. He takes pride in his ability to make his clients happy by finding percentages that work for them, so the logo reflects him personally as well as capturing the ethos of his firm.

Mr Wu uses an old-fashioned adding machine, which is alluded to by the die-cut edges of the business cards. The typographic treatment of the identity makes it clearly readable and further underscores the conceptual tie-in to the accuracy of the adding machine.

The design of the business cards continues the metaphor of the mechanical adding machine with custom-cut serrated edges at top and bottom. The phone number is divided by commas, like the totals in a financial statement.

The idea of turning a percentage sign into a smiley face came early on in the design process. Finding exactly the right percentage sign, however, involved the painstaking process of looking at the same symbol from 100 fonts or more.

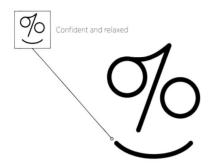

Confident and relaxed

PAUL
WU
+
ASSOCIATES
chartered accountants

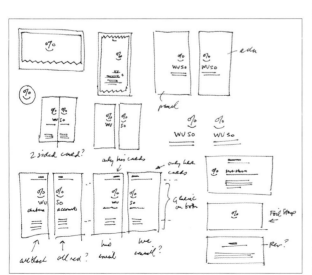

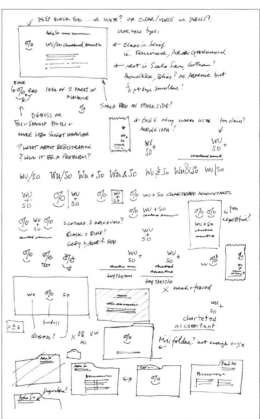

Many hand-drawn sketches went into the exploration phase of the design, in which a myriad of ideas were put on paper before the designer settled on the final one.

AGILITY

Sweating the details of a logo design is vital to achieving the right visual impact and the desired psychological effect

Brand story A merger of several Middle Eastern/Asian logistics and freight companies, with 20,000 employees in more than 100 countries, required a new brand for its management of supply chains, freight, defense and government services, fairs and events, and logistics

Studio Siegel+Gale

Creative director Sven Seger

Design director Marcus Bartlett

Designer Monica Chai

Typeface Cronos MM Italic (modified)

Colors Reds, oranges, and browns (process blends)

Design approach This newly formed corporation sought to establish a reputation for specialized, personal service and customized solutions. A global company, it nevertheless had a good understanding of local cultures. More than 80 names were considered, including made-up words, internal and industry ideas, and actual words from languages including English, Latin, Greek, and Arabic. Fortunately, the name Agility was already owned by one of the merging companies. Once the name was selected, a global symbol was needed to help tie it to the new company. The logo had to capture the notion of agility, reflect a dedication to people and cultures, and embody the idea of customized logistics solutions. The dragon is common to many cultures and is thought of as a symbol of strength, power, wisdom, and leadership—as well as being associated with trade. For an industry dominated by functional names—trans-, sped-, express, and the like—and icons of globes and trucks, this imaginative identity stands out, underscoring its brand values of leadership, flexibility, speed, determination, and cultural heritage.

Besides the logo and its variations, the identity includes a color system, style of imagery, typography for all uses from print to electronic, and a supplementary graphic motif to differentiate communications without overusing the logo. In a complex identity such as this, each element becomes a little system of its own.

The new identity, led by a distinctive and dramatic logo with a stylized dragon, was applied in contexts ranging from buildings to vehicles to stationery.

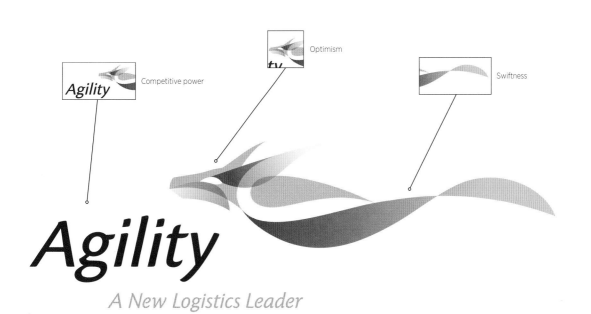

Competitive power

Optimism

Swiftness

Agility

A New Logistics Leader

Few identities exist where the name and the symbol engage in a dialogue that informs and strengthens one another.

We started off with Rotis Sans Italic. It felt neutral and made the symbol the hero. From the beginning, we knew we needed an italic face that had movement.

The strength in this identity is the dialogue between both the name and symbol—to do so, we looked at typefaces that had more personality such as Cronos MM Italic and Shaker.

After selecting Cronos MM Italic, we redrew each letter to have characteristics that imitated features in the symbol of the dragon.

Final logo

Modified from Rotis Sans Italic

Cronos MM Italic 574 SB 11 OP

Cronos MM Italic 574 SB 11 OP Modified

We used Cronos MM Italic to create one unit out of the name, symbol, and tagline.

Shaker Italic

Shaker Italic Modified

We further exaggerated the angle of the italic face to convey continuity as it met the symbol.

Even the dots in the "i" and the "g" were specifically drawn to accommodate the way the symbol appears in either direction on both sides of the trucks.

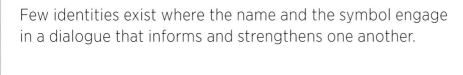

Although the client was very pleased with the initial version of the logo, as the process of rolling it out and applying the identity to all the myriad applications got underway, it became clear that certain slight modifications would be needed.

First, the facial features of the dragon were adjusted, with special focus on the shape of the eye, to make sure it expressed the desired personality for the brand perfectly. The original version was seen as too assertive. After exploring numerous alternatives, a variant with a more optimistic expression was chosen. The shape and angle of the dragon's body were subtly adjusted for the same reason. Finally, the exact letterforms of the name Agility were recrafted to make the font appear less generic and better integrated with the symbol. A few details were modified to imitate features of the dragon; there are even subtle left- and right-hand versions so that the sense of motion is realistic on both sides of a truck.

In addition to these tweaks to the design itself, a number of additional variants were worked up as it became clearer how the logo was working in the many contexts in which it had to be deployed: building signage, vehicle liveries, and so forth. Legibility and recognition in constrained spaces, at distances, and at night, were taken into consideration. In the end, multiple variants were adopted to ensure that the brand is always presented in the most appropriate way for the given context.

In addition to careful selection of the typeface, the details of the dragon's head and body were meticulously refined. Particular attention was given to the shape and position of the white eye, a natural (if subconscious) point of focus and therefore a crucial place to make sure the brand personality was properly expressed.

Our Top Three Designs & Recommendation

Recommended

Expression of Optimism

This design of the eye is a unique and distinctive combination of stability, energy and credibility. The large and even shape of the eye promotes stability, while the double points and generous curves speak to energy. The eye's position in the head is natural – a subtle expression of credibility.

Expression of Sincerity

This design is relevant and appropriate for Agility's dragon, but a slight upward curve on the top of the eye makes it feel a bit too passive and slow. While we like the idea of sincerity, its expression may not feel right for the dragon in combination with the notion of agility.

Expression of Friendship

This design of the eye is very warm, natural and approachable. The general ideas of hope and friendship are relevant to the company, but their expression in the eye of the dragon creates a visible sign of reservation, an aesthetic that while appropriate, does not reflect the notion of agility as well as the other designs.

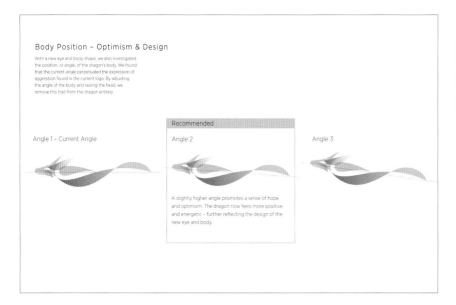

Body Position – Optimism & Design

With a new eye and body shape, we also investigated the position, or angle, of the dragon's body. We found that the current angle perpetuated the expression of aggression found in the current logo. By adjusting the angle of the body and raising the head, we remove this trait from the dragon entirely.

Angle 1 – Current Angle

Recommended

Angle 2

A slightly higher angle promotes a sense of hope and optimism. The dragon now feels more positive and energetic – further reflecting the design of the new eye and body.

Angle 3

The thickness and angle of the dragon's body were fine-tuned to give it the desired sense of dynamism and motion. Too thin or too fat would suggest a mean or lazy company; too flattened or too steeply rising would suggest an over-aggressive or self-interested company.

Option Overview & Comparison

Option 1

Option 2

Option 3

Option 4

Option 4B

Option 5

The adjusted dragon symbol was then matched with each of the font options to find the best overall solution.

Acceptable Formats

Agility

Preferred Format (Diagonal)

Agility

Alternate Format (Horizontal)

The final logo was prepared in two slightly different arrangements; the latter is used in contexts such as building signs where the vertical space is limited, to allow the greatest possible visibility of the name.

CHARTIS

A completely new identity and logo, rapidly developed, not for a start-up, but for a giant global corporation

Brand story   The AIG insurance business, although not involved in the problems of the Financial Products division, was suffering from a badly damaged image, and it was clear that a new brand was needed. Chartis is the new identity for 34,000 employees in 160 countries, serving more than 40 million customers

Studio   Lippincott

Art directors   Connie Birdsall and Alex de Jánosi

Designers   Daniel Johnston and James Yamada

Other   Fabian Diaz and Dolores Philips (environmental graphics); Suzanne Hogan, Sarah Bellamy, and Allen Gove (strategy); Jeremy Darty and Brendan deVallance (production)

Typeface   Bliss (redrawn)

Colors   Blue (PMS 2945) and yellow (Toyo CF 10165)

Design approach   In rare instances, it is better to throw out an old brand and start from scratch. After it became apparent that the AIG brand was a liability, a new brand was needed to win back customers' attention and build a clean platform for future growth.

Lippincott developed an entirely new brand identity program. Recent problems aside, the heritage of the organization includes a long history of exploration and taking on new challenges, being "global," and always striving to match an international reach with local understanding. The new identity conveys this. The company retains a strong innovative and entrepreneurial spirit, which is captured with a brand that feels true to the organization's internal culture, and functions as a rallying point for clients and employees.

Though it appears simple, type in the new logo was carefully adjusted by hand: its spacing suggests a new beginning, while subtle touches like the angled bar on the T convey optimism about the future. The icon, a tilted compass in the shape of a C, denotes the organization's pioneering spirit and symbolizes the brand's willingness to venture into new markets and products.

The new identity had to be applied quickly in many locations around the globe. Since it was impossible to map all the possible contexts in advance, the identity had to be simple and flexible in order to avoid creating unnecessary difficulties or adding extra costs.

Respectable

Established and stable

The compass symbol refers to the company's origins in Shanghai in 1919. Combined with a classic, simple typeface in blue, the logo instantly communicates reliability and global expertise.

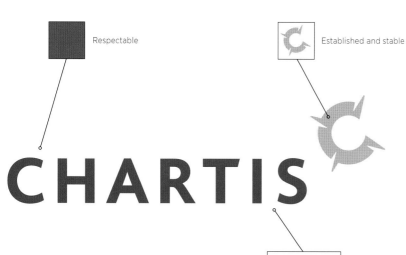

CHARTIS

CHARTIS Direction and purpose

Over time, the identity can be extended and used creatively as additional contexts are developed.

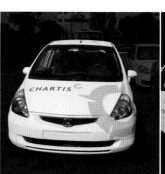

NONPROFIT & PUBLIC SECTOR

The public sector and nonprofit areas seem to offer by far the largest selection and diversity of design approaches of any group in this book. Perhaps it is because these organizations must focus on articulating their mission and vision to attract funding and support. These expressions of purpose are essentially brand statements or design briefs; having them clear from the outset makes a designer's job simpler and more rewarding.

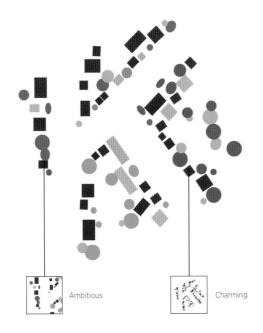

Ambitious

Charming

Client	Town of Kutina
Brand story	A small Croatian town of 15,000 seeking to attract sustainable technology development to replace its old petrochemical industry
Studio	Studio International
Designer	Boris Ljubicic
Typeface	[None]
Colors	Green, gray, and red
Design approach	Kutina is situated on an east–west road at the bottom of a wooded mountain, surrounded by green countryside. The purpose of the new identity was to position the town as an ideal place for clean and high-tech firms to move to. The initial K is turned into an idealized vision of a town plan amidst green surroundings; in the Croatian language, the word "kut" (the root of the town name) means corner, which reinforces the image of a charming, small-town crossroads in the many angles of the letter K.

The logo was rendered in several versions (as a 3D model and a flat plan, in positive and negative), and these are used interchangeably on various materials promoting the town. The competing versions reflect the complexity inherent in a municipal community and project a dynamic vision for the future: well organized, yet flexible; civilized, yet yearning for sustainable development

Humanistic

Futuristic

MINISTERSTVO VNITRA ČESKÉ REPUBLIKY

Client Interior Ministry of the Czech Republic

Brand story Nearly two decades after the end of Communism, the former Czechoslovakia's one-time "Ministry of Fear" seeks to reinvent itself as an open, modern government office committed to serving the people

Studio Lavmi

Designer Babeta Ondrová

Typeface Bespoke

Color Light blue (PMS 2995)

Design approach The Communist government's interior ministry (Ministerstvo Vnitra) had a reputation for spying on its own citizens and beating student protestors. When Czech elections in 2006 ushered in another change of government, political leaders decided to open up the ministry in the hope of burying its old reputation. An up-to-date public image was needed to reflect this new commitment to serving the people. The designers nested the initials M and V in a single shape. The negative space of the triangle alludes to the opening of doors, and with a little imagination the dots can be seen as people, or digital information. The bright sky blue reinforces the sense of turning away from a dark past

Client NERV (National Economic Council of the Czech Republic)

Brand story As a reaction to the worldwide financial crisis during 2008/2009, the Czech government established a public committee to advise on policy

Studio Lavmi

Designer Babeta Ondrová

Typeface Bespoke

Color Cyan (process color)

Design approach The council's mission was to find ways to prevent the global economic downturn from having too much negative impact on the country's economy and the everyday lives of Czech citizens. The designers looked for symbols that would convey the idea of protection and defense, and settled on an X. This sign alludes to telling trouble to "keep out," and also resembles a tilted version of the Red Cross, signifying the council's efforts to rescue the local economy. The council has 10 members, so, as the Roman numeral for 10, the X has another positive meaning

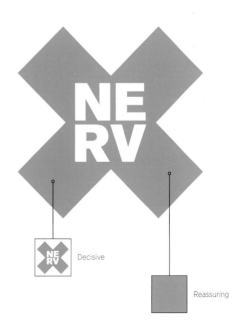

Decisive

Reassuring

Friendly

Serious

Client The Prince's Youth Business International (YBI)

Brand story A charity, supported by the Prince of Wales, that offers financial aid and mentoring to young entrepreneurs from underprivileged backgrounds

Studio The House

Art director Steven Fuller

Designer Sam Dyer

Typeface Monitor

Colors Blue (PMS 295) and orange (PMS 144)

Design approach The logo needed to communicate the synergy between YBI and various organizations around the world. It also needed to appeal to diverse audiences: young participants in their 20s and supporting partners of the charity who are generally older. Overall, the lowercase sans-serif type treatment gives the brand a youthful, approachable feel. The letterforms of the y and b echo each other, suggesting the aforementioned synergy, while the color scheme implies that a spark of energy and fun runs through the serious activities

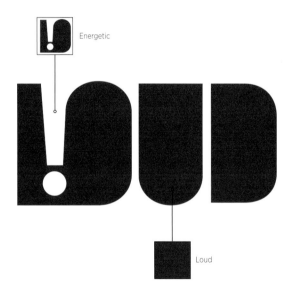

Energetic

Loud

Client LOUD Foundation

Brand story A Vancouver-based foundation for the gay, lesbian, bisexual, and transgender community

Studio Seven25. Design & Typography

Designer Isabelle Swiderski

Typeface Bespoke

Color Magenta (process color)

Design approach This logo design comes close to visual onomatopoeia: its form and color embody the meaning of the word " loud." It needed to appeal both to young people seeking scholarships and to potential donors and sponsors in the community at large. After rejuvenating the foundering organization with a new name (LOUD: Leadership, Opportunity, Unity, Diversity), the challenge was to define a brand personality that would be in keeping with its long-standing values. The visual solution was inspired by youth fashion and sports design, giving the brand a strong, relevant voice and a bold, recognizable identity reflective of the group's mission. The new logo helped raise substantial funds and convince sponsors to support the foundation again

Long-term

van∞uver
foundation

fo   Approachable

Client Vancouver Foundation

Brand story A foundation that facilitates long-term giving and endowments

Studio Seven25. Design & Typography

Designer Isabelle Swiderski

Typeface Bespoke, based on Avenir

Colors Gray (PMS 432) and blue (PMS 312)

Design approach The previous identity for this organization had a more traditional "old money" look. When the foundation decided it wanted to become more visible in the community, in order to better compete for charity contributions and move away from its largely behind-the-scenes role in funding other community groups, it needed a new identity to reflect that new role. The designer came up with a visual play on the middle letters of the city's name, based on an abstract concept of the continuous benefits of generous giving. The new look reflects the foundation's forward-thinking approach and makes it appear more accessible

er 🐝
cheste   Bold and recognizable

forever 🐝
manchester

Client Forever Manchester

Brand story A charity run by the Community Foundation for Greater Manchester, which funds projects across the city with the intention of making communities safer and more pleasant places to live

Studios Imagine-cga and Fido PR

Designer David Caunce

Contributors Laura Sullivan, Nancy Collantine, and Kate Pearson

Typeface Avant Garde Gothic Bold

Colors Red (PMS 485) and black

Design approach The design team wanted to capture the obvious ideas behind the fund, as reflected in the name—that giving represents an act of love for the city and that the benefits will be forever. The resulting mark also expresses the doubling of contributions under a government matching program, as well as the idea that those who give, receive benefits themselves, in the form of invitations, vouchers, and other perquisites. The bright-red icon also hints at a double M, and is strong and memorable enough to work with or without the name

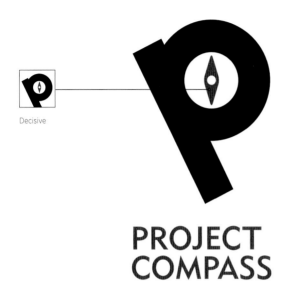

Decisive

PROJECT
COMPASS

Client Project Compass

Brand story A London-based charity offering direction to ex-servicemen, including job training and housing assistance

Studio Fivefootsix

Typeface Geometric

Colors Red (PMS 485) and black

Design approach The professional assistance offered by this organization is geared to helping servicemen recently out of the armed forces cope with getting reoriented into civilian life and work. The compass is instantly recognizable to an ex-serviceman as an essential tool for survival, so this icon speaks to its audience in a familiar visual language. The extra-bold P is reassuringly solid, imparting a sense of reliability, while its tilt hints at the sometimes challenging nature of life that the compass will help them navigate

Hopeful

Embracing and diverse

Phoenix House
Rising Above Addiction

Client Phoenix House

Brand story An addiction treatment center in New York City, USA

Studio Siegel+Gale

Creative director Doug Sellers

Designer Lana Roulhac

Typeface Rotis Serif

Colors Multicolored and black

Design approach The old logo for this nonprofit center, which helps people rise above their drug and alcohol dependency, looked dated and uninspiring. It failed to reflect the human stories of personal redemption and achievement that were playing out within the walls of Phoenix House and failed to motivate the staff and clientele. A new logo that could capture the simple, yet compelling aspirations of its residents was called for. The solution imparts a sense of the empowerment and joy that comes with kicking a destructive habit. The multicolored feathers reinforce both the name and the diversity of those who benefit—a racially and economically diverse group of New Yorkers

Client Home for the Games

Brand story An organization that arranges homestays for visitors to the Vancouver 2010 Winter Olympics, in aid of charities that fight homelessness

Studio Seven25. Design and Typography

Art director Isabelle Swiderski

Designer Setareh Shamdani

Typeface Bespoke

Colors Yellow, magenta, green, and blue, and their overlapping shades

Design approach The mark is celebratory and encouraging, representing the vigor of the organization and extending the spirit of the Olympic Games to its own charitable activities. Sports in general, and the Olympics in particular, have a rich visual language to draw on, and the designers used that to attract an audience of homeowners and visitors who wanted to celebrate the Olympics by extending its principle of brotherhood to a social cause. The boldly overlapping and geometric lettershapes allude to the Olympic rings without infringing on that carefully protected icon; the subtle heart shape within the M of HOME emphasizes the caring aspect

Festive

Energetic

Client Julian House (Cecil Weir)

Brand story A UK charity benefiting homeless men and women in Bath and the surrounding counties

Studio The House

Art director Steve Fuller

Designer Sam Dyer

Typeface DIN 17 SB Regular

Colors Blues (PMS 2955, PMS 7467)

Design approach The problem with the previous identity for this charity was that it didn't convey the full range of services offered to its clientele, which includes many support activities in addition to shelter for the night. This revision not only brings the brand a more modern and sophisticated look, the nested houses/arrows also signify a more diverse range of service offerings, making clear that the organization is progressive and well run

Progressive

Chabadum
Jewish Student Central

Dynamic and assertive

Client	Chabad at the University of Miami
Brand story	Part of an international organization bringing Jewish living to life
Designer	Marc Rabinowitz
Typeface	Helvetica Neue LT Black
Colors	Orange (PMS 151), green (PMS 375), and 80% black
Design approach	Chabad works in a decentralized manner; local groups are free to develop their own identities to suit their needs. While talking with the designer, the rabbi for the student group at the University of Miami campus mentioned that Chabad brings Jewish life to the heart of the University: this idea led to the graphic solution of a star embedded between two letters. This simplicity allows for a flexible, extended range of applications

Embracing and welcoming

Bethel Assembly of God

Client	Bethel Assembly of God
Brand story	A church in West Virginia, USA, with no previous logo wanted a graphic identity to help it reach out to its own members as well as the surrounding community
Studio	Church Logo Gallery
Designer	Michael Kern
Typeface	Labtop Secundo Regular
Colors	Orange (PMS 138), red (PMS 1807), and gray (PMS 439)
Design approach	In the Bible, a flame is one of the symbols of the Holy Spirit. The initial B, in its lowercase form, lends itself to the form of a flame as well as a person raising their arms in praise, the idea being that a person can be changed through faith in God. The warm colors create an inviting, welcoming feel and the resulting identity is easily recognizable and memorable. The logo is strong enough conceptually that its designer offers it for sale on his website to any church that would like to buy it. Local churches may not require a unique or exclusive identity as a larger church would

Joy and inclusiveness

Client	Explore Children's Ministry
Brand story	A church program aimed at children aged 5 to 11, encouraging them to be adventurous and to learn about the Christian faith
Studio	Church Logo Gallery
Art director	Michael Kern
Designer	Zach DeYoung
Typeface	Trade Gothic Extended
Colors	Red-orange, brown, and blue
Design approach	Making the identity for this program amusing and informal gives a sense of play and exploration. Says Michael Kern, "Kids will give it a try if it looks interesting and fun." The warm colors build up an expectation of excitement, while the blue circle surrounding the cross hints at the mysteries of faith waiting to be discovered

Sophisticated and savvy

Client	Grace Community Church
Brand story	A new church starting up in South Austin, Texas, USA, trying to reach out to people who don't already go to church, in an area where many other churches already compete for their attention
Studio	Virginia Green Design
Designer	Virginia Green
Typeface	Granjon
Colors	Red (PMS 1795) and black
Design approach	The logo had to look contemporary and make an impression on an audience that is already media-savvy and resistant to conventional marketing messages. One challenge was to come up with a mark that communicated a strong message of salvation, without using timeworn symbols such as a cross or a Bible. The word "Grace" was chosen for its special meaning to Christians and because its letters offer opportunities for manipulation. The red swash represents the blood of Christ and the completeness that one attains from being in a state of grace

Dynamic

Interconnected

Client	Red AIEP
Brand story	A research network, based at the University of Alcala de Henares in Spain, devoted to researching and preserving the written memories of people
Studio	CGB
Designer	Carol García del Busto
Typeface	Bespoke
Colors	Reds, in various shades from pale to deep
Design approach	The designer sought to represent the interaction between a large group of researchers, writers, collectors, teachers, librarians, and archivists working on a number of closely linked projects. The mark suggests the leaves of a book or a sheaf of letters, alluding to the written aspect of the work; the four directions show the variety of interconnected projects while the colors reinforce the name. The resulting logo has a strong and memorable impact

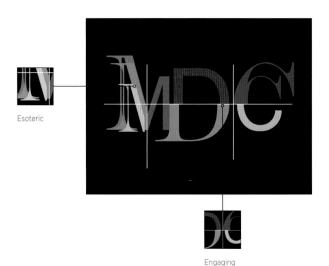

Esoteric

Engaging

Client	Museum Documentation Center
Brand story	A public-sector organization dedicated to gathering, organizing, and making accessible the documentary resources related to Croatia's museum collections
Studio	Studio International
Designer	Boris Ljubicic
Typefaces	DeVine and Helvetica (Swiss 721)
Colors	Multicolored
Design approach	The initials of this organization, MDC, are the same for the English and Croatian versions of the name. The designer decided to make the letters the centerpiece of the identity, using two diverse typefaces to reflect the timespan of the organization's activities, from early Romanesque artifacts to twentieth-century media and technology. The type is bisected by fine lines to form a checkerboard, an allusion to the red-and-white squares of the Croatian coat of arms. Half of each letter is in one font, half in the other. To ensure that this complex logo would still "read" in various media contexts and at small sizes, the designers prepared several versions with different degrees of contrast in color and size of the letters

Client Center for Cognitive Computing

Brand story A group researching the science of cognitive computing

Studio MINE

Art director/ Designer Christopher Simmons

Typeface [None]

Color Cyan (process color)

Design approach The designers aimed to avoid the clichés associated with many fringe sciences, such as robots or symbols of artificial intelligence. The mark is essentially formed by the repetition of many C's, and the effect of the Spirograph-like pattern, combined with faded edges, is to suggest movement at the periphery and signify an active brand

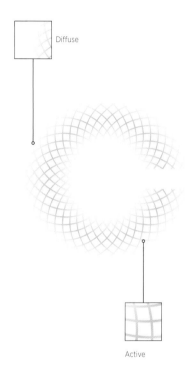

Diffuse

Active

Client Family Art Affair

Brand story A studio event for families at the Columbus Museum in Georgia, USA

Designer Andy Gabbert

Typeface Berthold Akzidenz Grotesk Extra Bold Condensed and Light Condensed

Colors Green (PMS 556), yellow (PMS 722), red (PMS 1805), and black

Design approach The logo needed to appeal to children and parents alike, so the challenge for the designer was to come up with a logo concept that wasn't too childish. The palette isn't strictly primary colors—it uses green and sand and a deep red instead of the more obvious blue, yellow, and red—and the choice of typefaces is more grown-up than it could have been. The contrast between extra bold and extra thin, and the rotation of the colors, together with the slight overlap tying the initials together, conveys an embrace of diversity and the idea that doing art together can help families bond

family art affair

Lighthearted and family oriented

Scholarly

Literary

Client	Siece, University of Alcares de Henares
Brand story	A university entity devoted to research and the study of written cultural history
Agency	CGB
Designer	Carol García del Busto
Typeface	Bespoke
Colors	Black and red
Design approach	The goal was to communicate the group's interest in written history clearly and directly to its audience of academic specialists, researchers, and students of humanities. The main design challenge was to show writing in the sense of typography rather than calligraphy. Colors were a key part of the solution, since red and black have traditionally been used for writing. The inspiration was old-fashioned writing implements—quills, inkwells, and so on—but also metal foundry type. The solution integrates these two elements in a logo that feels contemporary

Scholarly

Client	Center for Teaching Excellence (CTE) at the University of California, Berkeley, Haas School of Business
Brand story	CTE works with the university faculty to deliver high-quality classroom instruction through workshops and resources
Designer	Andy Gabbert
Project manager	Erica Mohar
Typeface	Filosofia
Color	Metallic bronze (PMS 8021 or PMS 451), and khaki (PMS 5803)
Design approach	The building-block symbol identifies the Center's activities as providing a foundation for quality teaching, while the gold palette reinforces the idea of distinction and achievement. The spaced, slab-serif type conveys a conservative feel typical of a high-level academic environment

Reminder that children will be well cared for

Crisp and professional

Client	Westboro Nursery School
Brand story	Childcare facility in Ottawa, Canada, that focuses on quality, professionalism, security, and care for the children entrusted to it
Studio	idApostle
Designer	Steve Zelle
Typeface	Century Schoolbook
Colors	Red-orange (PMS 1655) and black
Design approach	The designer chose to steer away from imagery of children at play to convey more of a preparatory message. The heart in the letter W obviously reinforces the idea of love. The addition of a little toning to the middle stroke of the W gives an impression of a single, continuous line crossing over and under itself, alluding to the ongoing process of education as part of life's journey

Modernity within tradition

Client	St. George's Academy
Brand story	A secondary school in Leicestershire, England
Studio	Planet
Art directors	Phil Bradwick and Christopher Higgins
Designers	Bobbie Haslett and Phil Bradwick
Typeface	ITC Avant Garde
Colors	Purple (PMS 268) and beige (PMS 9080)
Design approach	The school wanted to portray itself as well established in the context of the area's religious, agricultural, and medieval history, while also presenting a modern and professional image. The town in which the school is located is physically and socially centered on a medieval church, so the design team at Planet took their inspiration from its large stained-glass windows. The school had used Saint George and the dragon in its identity before, so this symbol was given a modern makeover. The old logo used primary colors and had many clashing elements. The designers lifted the important elements, simplifying and updating them, and softening the tones to a more cohesive palette of purples and grays

Vitality

Optimism

Client	TurnAround
Brand story	A nonprofit organization that partners with low-performing public schools in New York City to diagnose and fix problems in order to improve academics, safety, and the social environment
Studio	Siegel+Gale
Creative director	Doug Sellers
Designers	Lana Roulhac and Jong Woo Si
Typeface	VAG Rounded (modified)
Colors	Gray, green, dark blue, and purple
Design approach	Siegel+Gale took a lead role in crafting TurnAround's brand story in order to elevate its visibility and reputation, making it more effective in transforming some of the most disadvantaged schools and the lives of the children in them. The new identity brings to life the tenacity and optimism of the organization with its friendly, uplifting letterforms and bold palette of deep, contrasting colors that suggest the energy needed to make the best of a tough situation. To reward audiences that take a second look, the joyful figure of a child can be seen jumping up in the green u and n

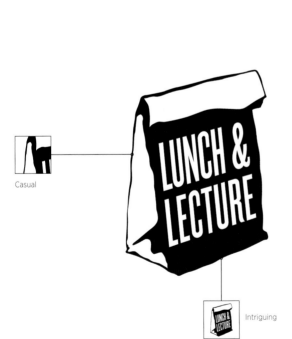

Casual

Intriguing

Client	Lunch & Lecture
Brand story	A program bringing visitors into an art museum for lunchtime lectures
Designer	Andy Gabbert
Typeface	Grotesque Extra Condensed
Colors	Black and white
Design approach	Most of the attendees at these "bring your own lunch" lectures are professionals who work in the downtown area near the Columbus Museum and want an inspiring and informative lunch break. The paper bag is a widely recognized symbol of an informal meal event, but by rendering it in dramatic black-and-white form, it takes on a sense of anticipation that turns it into an inviting logo

Client   Pilotprojekt

Brand story   A gallery space in Vienna conceived as a link between creative types and industry, where an open transfer of knowledge and ideas can occur

Designer   Alexander Egger

Typeface   Helvetica

Color   Black

Design approach   The letters PP are formed by a pair of lines and circles, two of the most elementary devices for defining space and dimension. The visual language of the identity is extremely minimal, taking the philosophy that the space is a structure operating in the background and needs no color or decorative elements of its own. Its spare style makes reference to the historical design movements of the Bauhaus and constructivism, in which design was more a sociopolitical tool than a system of aesthetics. The logo is arranged with the two lowercase words, "pilot" and "projekt," along various grids to introduce some variation to the layouts that use it and to make clear the connections that underlie the gallery's programs

pilot projekt

Formal and structured

Client   International Private Schools Integrated Systems (IPSIS)

Brand story   A school system that focuses on the individual student at the same time that it provides a grounding for collective school spirit and community

Studio   PenguinCube

Designers   PenguinCube design team

Typeface   Wunderlich (modified)

Colors   Blues (tints of PMS 2735)

Design approach   The logo needed to be applied on an international level and also to be developed into a clear and easy-to-use system with variations for subgroups within IPSIS. The visual inspiration was the idea of a seal of confidence and trust, referencing traditional wax letter seals. This particular seal incorporates an element of fun and speaks to both children and adults, giving the brand a bold, clear signature that remains recognizable even when the nomenclature changes in different parts of the system

IPSIS
International Private
Schools Integrated Systems

Confidence and trustworthiness

TENTH CHURCH

The brand-identity needs of a religious organization are scarcely different from those of a corporation

Brand story   A large and growing congregation serving a diverse urban community in Vancouver, Canada

Studio   Nancy Wu Design

Designer   Nancy Wu

Typefaces   Gotham Bold, with minor modifications, and Locator Medium

Colors   Black, augmented by a second color for sub-brands: orange, blue, or green

Design approach   A typical "soft" church-heritage style was rejected in favor of a look that reflected the modern, urban approach of this diverse church and the need to project an authentic image. Ms Wu explains that "the simple wordmark incorporates a graphic icon with multiple conceptual themes of worship, welcome, transformation, outreach, and the cross."

A flexible identity system was also required to identify two different locations and an alternative evening service. The church had expanded beyond its original Tenth Avenue location, but retained that history in its name. The new identity also had to appeal both to the existing members and to the community at large. The contexts in which the logo would appear included the extremes of large signs and small ads in local newspapers, along with some unusual applications such as embroidery on clothing.

The communication needs of a church can be just as complex as those of a corporation, so the logo required the same care with its crafting, from articulating the concept in a design brief to crafting the details of the final rendition.

Ms Wu says the old logo was "difficult to read, challenging to reproduce, lacking a clearly accessible concept, and arguably too abstract or feminine in nature." To depart from this, the client brief requested that the new brand reflect a bold, modern, masculine image that would also accurately capture the varied and inclusive demographic of the church community. The type treatment was chosen for its appropriateness, readability, and style: modern, but not so much that it would quickly become dated.

The church organization needed a clear, consistent identity to use in all its communications, as well as on items that members of the congregation could wear to show their affinity. A graphically simple, bold, and modern solution was the most appropriate.

TENTHC — Dynamic and down-to-earth

TEN†HCHURCH

 Trustworthy and accessible

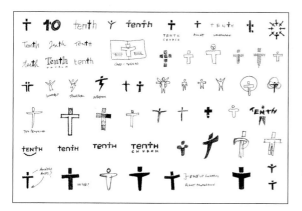

TEN†HCHURCH
3RD SERVICE

TEN†HCHURCH
KITSILANO

TEN†HCHURCH
MT PLEASANT

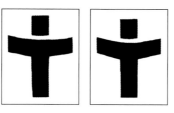

Even though the final logo appears simple and unassuming, a great deal of design work went into developing and refining it. The concept of turning the letter T into a cross/Christ figure could be approached in numerous ways, and finding the right one required a disciplined process of trying out many variations. The final selection balances a distinctive icon and legibility within the word "Tenth." After the basic logo was resolved, an elegant way of using color to extend the name for the church's sub-brands was found.

10TH
TEN†H
†TENTH
10†h
TEN†H
TEN†H
TEN†H
TEN†H

TEN†H CHURCH MT PLEASANT
TEN†H CHURCH KITSILANO
TEN†H CHURCH MT PLEASANT
TEN†H CHURCH KITSILANO

ten†h

Cross:
- as a bridge (visual & spiritual)
- as a place of worship
- as a symbol of Christ
- as a welcoming figure (person)
- as a visible bold graphic

People = community
Open arms = inclusive
Green = growing

CITY OF MELBOURNE

An edgy, vibrant design concept that captures the personality of a large, diverse, urban community

Brand story A diverse, multicultural city in Australia offering its inhabitants and visitors world-class culture, education, and shopping

Studio Landor Associates

Creative director Jason Little

Designers Jason Little, Sam Pemberton, Ivana Martinovic, Jefton Sungkar, and Malin Holmstrom

Others Cable Daniel-Dreyfus, James Cockerille, and Katie Crosby (strategists); Amanda Lawson (client director); Joao Peres, Jason Little, and Chenying Hao (photographers)

Typefaces Bespoke, based on Arete (full identity uses Mercury and Gotham)

Colors Full spectrum

Design approach Fifteen years had passed since the city council last commissioned a graphic identity, and multiple logos had accumulated for various city services and offices making it hard (and costly) to manage, and presenting a confusing face to the public. The council knew it needed a better long-term solution and turned to Landor for a cohesive brand strategy and a fresh identity system.

The challenge was to reflect the cool sophistication of Melbourne, to express the passion of its people, and to provide an image that would work in a unified, flexible way, bringing together all the programs, services, events, tourist destinations, and political entities under one umbrella.

After research that included assessing public opinion and talking to business owners, public officials, and community representatives, Landor's designers came up with a complex branding program. Its centerpiece is a bold M, multifaceted like the city it represents and able to give full expression to the diversity and personal energy of its inhabitants. As an icon, it is immediately recognizable by its outline; as a vehicle for communicating the city's brand, it can be endlessly reinvented, reinterpreted, and recycled. It is an identity that Landor likes to call sustainable and "future-proof."

The concept gave the design team the flexibility to produce dozens of variations on the logo, providing unified, but distinctive sub-brand identities for the many organizations and programs that needed them.

Dynamic and multicultural

CITY OF MELBOURNE

From large outdoor posters to online pages and small publications, the identity is instantly recognizable, with an impact that captures—and contributes to—the exciting atmosphere of a modern, diverse city.

The concept also encompasses secondary graphic motifs derived from some of the patterns used in the logo itself.

ENVIRONMENT

As environmental awareness spreads and markets all over the world demand greener brands, environmentally related branding has become fully mainstream. Logos in this area are shedding the old visual clichés and exploring the same design innovations as other sectors. Certain conventions (for example, green leaves) remain; otherwise, designs for environmental organizations, destinations, and causes are as vibrant, and surprising, as any.

Simple and clean

Client	One Degree
Brand story	An internal program, begun in 2007, to encourage employees of News Corporation to help the company become carbon neutral within three years
Studio	Landor Associates
Creative director	Jason Little
Designers	Jason Little, Mike Rigby, Angela McCarthy, Steve Clarke, and Tim Warren
Typeface	VAG Rounded
Colors	Cyan (process color) and black
Design approach	In 2007, Rupert Murdoch announced that News Corporation would aim to reduce its net carbon output to zero by 2010. However, since the company already had a long history as an environmental leader in the media industry, it didn't want to appear as if it were simply jumping on the green bandwagon. The strategy and design team at Landor came up with a clear, simple brand name and logo that convey a feeling of empowerment (not guilt) to give employees the sense that each of them can make a real difference. The logo, in which the number 1 and the degree symbol represent each employee making a small difference every day, can be replicated to show cooperative effort as well.

The internal program was successful. News Corporation's environmental officer reported that One Degree is regarded within the media industry as a leading example of employee communication on environmental responsibility. Ninety-five percent of News Corporation employees participate, keeping the company on track to meet its goals

Client Northwest Hub

Brand story An independent, online news site providing analysis on environmental, land use, and real estate issues in the Pacific Northwest of the USA. Its mission is to connect the fields of architecture, engineering, planning, land use and environmental law, real estate, transportation, and urban design

Studio Riverbed Design

Designer Corbet Curfman

Typefaces Frutiger Bold and Extra Black

Colors Greens (PMS 7495, PMS 7492, and PMS 7477)

Design approach The goal of the website is to be innovative in selecting subjects and delivering news. One challenge in crafting an identity was to portray something specific to the audience about subject matter, without being seen as attached to just one group. A purely typographic treatment would have been the easy way out, but a pictorial or symbolic element makes the logo easier to "read," especially in the context of a busy website. The skyline and mountain range are a good compromise, communicating at several levels and covering all Northwest Hub's areas of interest, while also avoiding clichés such as the symbolic leaf. Arranging the elements into a compact square allows the logo to function at lower resolutions, as an icon or avatar in social media and mobile applications

Environmentalism

Convenience

Depth and richness of information

Playful

Engaging; triggers the
imagination

Client	Design Stories/Uppvunnet
Brand story	An exhibition of furniture and product design that uses recycled materials, held in Sweden
Designers	Emilia Lundgren and Karolina Wahlberg Westenhoff
Typeface	Photographs of letterforms made using trash items—magazines, paper cups, and discarded packaging—found in the streets
Colors	Multicolored
Design approach	The Swedish word uppvunnet means "upcycled," and the logo reflects this by recycling bits of graphic design items. The logo was used on posters, invitations, and the web. As it wasn't to be used at small sizes, many of the design constraints of a traditional logo were removed. Ms. Lundgren says, "Every graphic solution that diminishes the amount of waste around us, and makes us use our hands instead of our computers, is important for the environment and for our future"

Repetition hints
at reuse

Client	Re:cycle
Brand story	An exhibition about sustainability in packaging design that took place at designforum in Vienna
Studio	Satellites Mistaken for Stars
Designer	Alexander Egger
Typeface	Bespoke
Colors	Green (PMS 376) and black
Design approach	The logo doubles up the name of the exhibition, with the full name on the middle line symbolizing a cyclical return without the use of clichéd arrows. Through modifications to make it look like a stencil, the typeface takes on a temporary character, like packaging itself, and the arrangement of the words alludes to the ongoing discussion about sustainability. To promote the exhibition, the logo was used as the basis for a repeating pattern, suggestive of mass production. Paper printed with this pattern was wrapped around a 3D model of the venue logo and around traffic signs and benches near the exhibition, and these were photographed for use on posters and invitations

Client	Go Green
Brand story	The Sacred Heart Cathedral Preparatory School in California wanted to encourage students to be conscious of paper consumption in particular, and the environment in general
Studio	MINE
Designers	Christopher Simmons and Tim Belonax
Typeface	MetroScript (modified)
Colors	Greens (PMS 343, PMS 367, and PMS 355)
Design approach	Since Go Green is really a tagline rather than the name of a product or service, the lettering style needed to exude enthusiasm. It was also convenient to link it visually to the school's Irish heritage, playing on the similarity between the traditional recycling arrows and the green leaves of popular Irish iconography. The result is a memorable logotype the school can consider its own; it references recycling, but is original enough to avoid cliché

Fun

Energetic

Client	Garbage Critic
Brand story	Waste reduction consulting services for corporations and government agencies
Studio	Seven25. Design & Typography
Designer	Isabelle Swiderski
Typeface	Helvetica Light
Colors	Green and black
Design approach	The main challenge was to express the company's central activity clearly and in an appealing fashion. "Garbage is not sexy," says the designer, Isabelle Swiderski. Nevertheless, by thinking about the services in terms of a puzzle metaphor, she was able to come up with a solution that is "simple, specific, and a little bit clever," all qualities that describe the company well

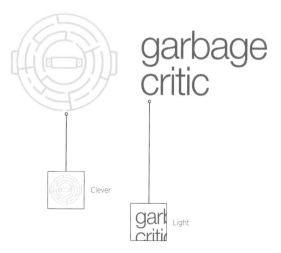

Clever

Light

Contemporary

WILDCRU
Wildlife Conservation Research Unit

Clever

Client	WildCRU (Wildlife Conservation Research Unit)
Brand story	Founded in 1986, WildCRU was the first university-based conservation research unit in Europe. Based at Oxford University, it aims to bridge the gap between academic theory and practical problem solving
Studio	Inaria
Creative director	Andrew Thomas
Designers	Andrew Thomas and Naomi Mace
Typeface	Avenir (modified)
Colors	Sienna (PMS 1675) and brown (PMS 7505)
Design approach	The brief for this logo design was to replace the old icon (a circle of type surrounding a woodcut illustration of a fox leaping onto a field mouse) with something more contemporary and professional. The solution was to combine symbols of what the organization does—researching and disseminating information—with the distinctive shape of a fox's head, since the red fox was recognized and liked by everyone familiar with the old logo. The crisp, sans-serif type makes the required contemporary statement. To improve readability, a second hue is used for the half-word, half-initials name

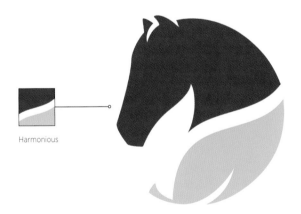

Harmonious

Client	San Francisco Parks Trust
Brand story	New, ecologically friendly stables at Golden Gate Park
Studio	MINE
Art directors	Christopher Simmons and Kate Earhart
Designer	Kate Earhart
Typeface	[None]
Colors	Light green (PMS 390) and brown-black (PMS Black 7)
Design approach	This design solution fulfills all of the classic criteria for a logo—it is compact, bold, simple, distinctive, and recognizable. It elegantly incorporates the horse's head and leaf into a circle, creating a simple icon that conveys the subject and can be used easily in almost any context. It is beautifully proportioned and makes use of a modern, understated palette of natural colors that reinforce its expression of the park environment and the natural harmony it seeks to promote

Client	Hong Kong Wetland Park
Brand story	A wetland reserve with a visitor center that includes galleries, theater, store, play area, and resource center
Studio	Executive Strategy Ltd.
Art directors	Ng Lung-wai and Ben Poon Ho-sing
Designer	Jasmine Ho
Typeface	Helvetica
Colors	Spectrum of 20 hues, from green to red
Design approach	The visitor center needed a visual system to demonstrate the diversity of Hong Kong's fragile wetland ecosystem and the need for preserving it. Each wetland species displays a unique adaptation, but it is their interaction as part of a complex web of life that makes the environment special. This is reflected in the series of stamp designs, depicting 20 species, which visitors to the center can collect. Their delicate style conveys the fragility of the wetlands; their common shape and the unifying spectrum of color underscore their interdependence. The logos are also applied to a wide range of souvenirs and print items

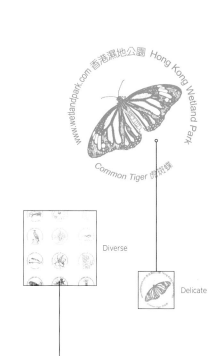

Common Tiger 虎斑蝶

Diverse

Delicate

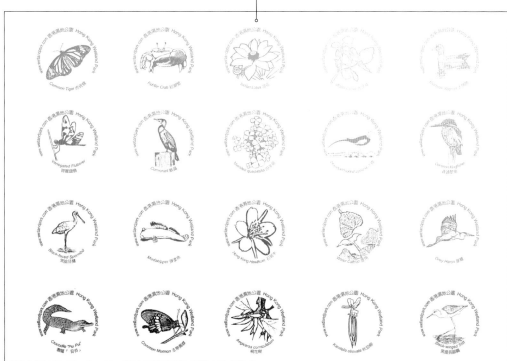

NORTH SHORE SPIRIT TRAIL

Branding the outdoors can help make the natural world more accessible to humanity, and humanity more appreciative of the natural world

Brand story   A sustainable, multiuse waterfront pathway stretching for 23¾ miles (35km) from west to north Vancouver, Canada, allowing people to walk, run, skate, or bike the newly developed trails of Vancouver's North Shore

Studio   Seven25. Design & Typography

Creative director   Isabelle Swiderski

Designer   Nancy Wu

Typeface   Gotham

Colors   Red (PMS 7420) and gray (PMS Cool Gray 11)

Design approach   The new mark was intended to symbolize not just the community groups that created the path, but also the heritage of the Squamish Nation native to the area that participated in the development of the trail. Aimed at both residents and visitors using the path for recreation, and people using the trail to get to work, the logo would have a variety of applications, including being carved in wood or sandblasted out of rock. Without falling into inappropriate clichés typical of tourist graphics, the designer looked to cues from Native art and came up with a gender-neutral figure named Stelmelxo (Slomoh), Squamish for "person of the land."

The simple, hand-drawn figure combines the human form, the pathway, and the letter S, effectively conveying the simple beauty of the outdoors and a healthy lifestyle in a way that respects both the users and the natural location.

One of the hallmarks of a successful logo designer is their ability to set aside even very good preliminary designs in favor of a concept that fulfills its strategic brand goals, in this case getting more people to use the trail.

The logo needed to be simple in form so it could be applied easily to natural sign materials such as wood and stone, and be recognizable even from a distance. Although the androgynous figure appears crudely drawn, she/he was the product of lengthy experimentation to get the strokes just right, conveying the desired sense of energy, optimism, and endurance.

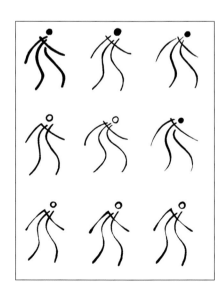

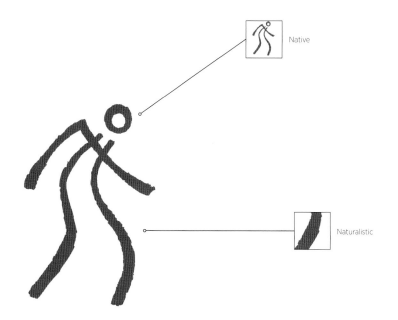

Native

Naturalistic

SPIRIT
TRAIL

Among the rejected designs are some good visual
ideas based on leaves, fish, and pathways. It is easy
to see how these visual explorations led to the final
icon, which incorporates hints of all three, but has
stronger emotional appeal because of its clearly
human element.

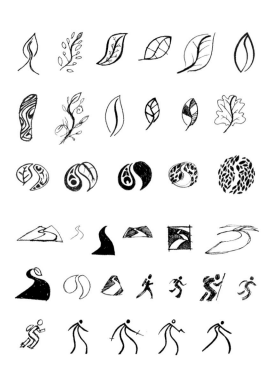

FOCUS ON ...

Taken as a group, the examples on the preceding pages demonstrate several trends in logo design. First, it's clear that logo design is a flourishing business in countries where Arabic, Cyrillic, Chinese, and other scripts are used. This offers designers new challenges: incorporating multiple alphabets into a logo, or creating an icon that "reads" equally well in reverse. It also means that multicultural sensitivities are important as never before: shapes and colors need to be contemplated through different sets of eyes.

Certain style trends of the 1990s, like the "layered" and "constructed" looks spawned by desktop illustration software, seem to have faded away. In their place, a simpler iconography has returned, which, whether stylistic or conceptual, relies more on communicating a brand idea than on acting as a showcase of computer skills.

Meanwhile, some old rules of logo design seem to have been, if not discarded, at least permanently amended. Advances in technology, and our shifting cultural tastes, now make concepts that were once unthinkable quite normal. A letterhead with 22 colors? No problem. Seven gradations simultaneously on the side of a truck? Push the button. A typeface that's terribly hard to read? Just what the client asked for.

Nonetheless, the DNA of logo design hasn't really changed. Rules still exist, and they generally help designers liberate their creativity rather than restricting what can be done. Keeping these rules in mind will make it easier to execute the design process successfully, and more likely that the final design will be satisfactory to everyone.

... FORM & SHAPE

Most icons can be categorized into one of a few basic shapes: circle, triangle, square, rectangle, cross, star, shield, and so forth. This is not as reductive as it may seem. Our eyes and brains have a natural tendency to simplify and mentally classify what we see according to what is familiar. That's how we make sense of our surroundings. Designers can take advantage of this. Logos that fall easily into a recognizable shape category are more memorable and easier to associate with positive brand values.

Experienced designers also understand that this tendency to categorize means that every logo shape naturally acquires some kind of nickname (even unconsciously) in the minds of its audience. It is useful for the brand if viewers are offered a logo design that gravitates naturally to a familiar category and a positive nickname. Logos that try too hard to appear original risk ending up with an ironic or derogatory nickname. In the worst case, this may run counter to the brand's ideas and values. Infamous examples include the NASA "meatball" logo, the Lucent "coffee stain" logo, and the London 2012 Olympics "swastika" logo.

By joining an iconic symbol to a brand name, a logo is created.

Organic

Wholly integrating

Client KAUST (King Abdullah University of Science and Technology, Saudi Arabia)

Brand story An international, graduate-level research university dedicated to inspiring a new age of scientific achievement

Agency Siegel+Gale

Creative director Justin Peters

Typeface Bespoke

Colors Red, blue, green, and orange-yellow

Design approach As the traditions of Islam discourage the representation of people, most Islamic art is nonfigurative, so abstract logo designs are ideal. Rather than alluding to anything specifically scientific or technical, the designers crafted a set of irregular circles, connected by overlaid concentric rings. The many symbolic meanings of this icon are readily apparent, and appropriate

KAUST
King Abdullah University of Science and Technology

Client Iskandar Malaysia

Brand story A region in southern Malaysia that hopes to develop into a sustainable, environmentally friendly metropolis within a few years

Studio Interbrand

Designer Karen Leong

Typeface Bespoke

Colors A changing palette of uncommon colors including orange, eggplant, turquoise, and lime-green

Design approach The design brief for this development zone called for emphasizing the combination of factors that make the region attractive for work, investment, and living. The triangles intrinsically symbolize wholeness, balance, and stability; the visual brand identity built with them is modular, allowing for a flexible communication system that can be adjusted for different audiences

Vibrant

Universal or culturally specific?

Do shapes have intrinsic meaning? Yes and no. The significance we ascribe to shapes, consciously or not, is, to some degree, universal and humanistic, and, to some degree, dependent on our specific cultures. In almost every culture a circle represents the continuity of life, a star represents a quest for power or eternity, a shield stands for strength and authority. But other symbols' meanings are more culturally dependent. The best-known (and perhaps the most extreme) example of culturally determined meaning is the starkly diverging significance of the hooked cross, or swastika. In Asia, the ancient Mediterranean, and Mesoamerica, it has represented eternal life and good fortune for millennia; in Western cultures it is impossible to forget its association with Nazism and the Holocaust.

Does a logo need a consistent shape, or indeed any shape at all? What about a constantly changing free-form logo that defies categorization? The Austrian-Italian designer Alexander Egger, for example, frequently deconstructs the standard notion of what a logo is and what purpose it serves. In the identity for the redhot marketing agency, each employee completes the logo by hand in his or her own unique way. This presentation of the identity supports the brand concept that redhot is a boutique firm delivering personally tailored solutions.

The swastika, or hooked cross, and six-pointed star have different meanings in Asia than in Europe or North America. Here the two symbols are combined on a centuries-old mandala from India, on which they represent life and hope.

Client	redhot
Brand story	Marketing and communications agency based in Austria
Designer	Alexander Egger
Typeface	Akkurat
Color	Red (PMS 213)
Design approach	Any time an employee hands out a business card or sends a letter, the logo must be filled in by hand. The initial R and the underline establish the space and provide a link between all representatives of the company, ensuring that they are part of a team; nevertheless, the logo never appears exactly the same way twice

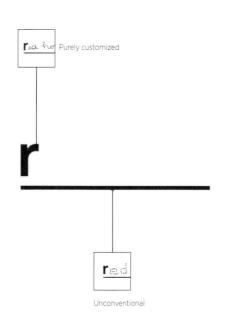

Purely customized

Unconventional

The most fundamental shape is a line. Because it is so basic, however, a line cannot hold much meaning and, therefore, must be turned into a more complex shape before it becomes a logo. The following eight basic shapes all have some universal meanings; many also have culturally specific meanings beyond those mentioned here. Of course, there are shapes beyond the eight listed below. Human and animal shapes are popular in logo design, as are natural forms such as leaves, but many of these are abstracted or stylized in such a way that they become circles, squares, or triangles. Some logo shapes are also hard to put into just one category. Although our brains find it easier to remember something if we can label it, shapes that defy ready classification also intrigue us, and become memorable in that way.

Circle

Circular, or nearly circular shapes are the most organic. Rendered with depth, they become spherical or globular. Circles and globes remind us of the sun and moon, eggs, and droplets of water, and because of this, they are often used to symbolize the life cycle. More abstractly, a circle symbolizes the turning of the seasons, the unity of the world, or the "music of the spheres." Arcs and crescents—parts of a circle—symbolize the heavens, or the flight of an object, and represent security, protection, trust, and faith. A figure 8 (two interconnected circles) is a common symbol for infinity.

Square

Perfect squares seldom occur in nature, but they are the most basic shape drawn by humans. The square and the cube represent order, rationality, and establishment of control over the natural elements. The rectangle—or elongated square—forms the basis of most compositions: the "golden ratio" established by the ancient Greeks is the most visually satisfying and can be found again and again in Western art and architecture, as well as in graphic design. Many logotypes are arranged into invisible "golden rectangles."

Triangle

Whether equilateral or isosceles, right-angle or oblique, the triangle is often used to establish a sense of constructive tension in a composition. Nature prefers pairs and circles, so our brains often struggle, unconsciously, to resolve a triangular shape into something simpler. Triangles and pyramids command our attention and have been used to represent authority, conflict, and sexuality. As arrows, triangles are universal indicators of direction.

Cross

A cross, the intersection of two lines in whatever proportion, is the next most common symbol. In ancient times crosses symbolized intersection, the four points of the compass, and the abstraction of the human figure. In many cultures a hooked cross, alone or along a zigzag line, symbolizes the continuity of life and good fortune. In Western cultures an upright cross represents Christianity and its rituals.

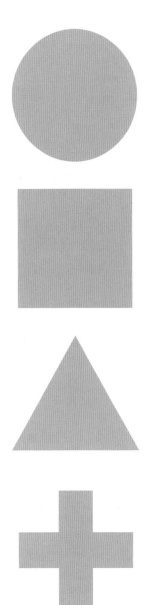

Star

Five, six, seven, eight ... however many points they have, stars are among the most romantic and inspiring of our symbols, as well as the most popular in logos and trademarks. Stars symbolize eternity, hope, energy, faith, freedom, and the quest for life. Their ubiquity and their use to represent widely diverging, even opposing concepts make them perhaps the most paradoxical of symbols.

Diamonds, pentagons, and hexagons

Some diamonds are squares or parallelograms rotated 45°, while others are irregular pentagons, resembling the cut stones used in jewelry. The symbolic meanings of diamonds tend to be more culturally specific than universal, but they often represent refinement, quality, or luxury. Hexagons, because of their natural ability to form a beehive cell pattern, can be used to represent networks or social structures.

Spiral

The cross-section of a nautilus shell is a well-known image because of its beautiful proportions and mathematical regularity, but there are other types of spirals as well. They fascinate us because they can go inward and outward forever. Spirals can represent infinity, the mystery of life, the natural order of the universe, and the serenity and solemnity of nature.

Shield

The most artificial of the major shape categories, shields can come in many varieties, derived from classical or modern armor designs. Often an amalgam of squares, triangles, and circles, they represent security, protection, strength, and authority. Interestingly, their association is often more with peace than with conflict. The human face is essentially a shield shape.

... COLOR

Although the technology of color reproduction today allows print in almost any hue, tint, or gradation, on almost any kind of surface, and LCD and plasma displays offer incredible saturation and brightness, a great many logos are still designed in plain old black and white.

Sometimes this is a matter of necessity—some contexts for presenting a logo, such as faxes or low-tech digital displays, still have technical limits on color use—but more often, a logo is designed in black and white for aesthetic reasons. Numerous examples in this book show that the preferred solution was the simple, fundamental contrast of a chiaroscuro icon, giving the logo a stark, chic, modern appeal.

In many more cases, a black-and-white version is but a starting point for a range of colorful applications and variants. Many experienced designers begin sketching their ideas with a pencil, trying to determine the optimal form and composition for the symbol without the distractions of texture, color, dimensionality, or typography. There is a traditional belief, and it is one still held by many designers, that if an icon doesn't work in black-and-white, it won't work in color. On the other hand, there are plenty of logos in this book that work precisely because of the way they exploit color. If rendered in monochrome, they would lose a vital element of their success. There are obviously many designers who launch themselves into the design process by experimenting not with form, but with color, and the logos that result are not so much a shape as a composition in hue and tone.

Designers choose colors carefully for their meanings and associations, using them subtly to help tell a story and craft an experience. Naturally, no single approach can resolve all design issues in all contexts. It is necessary to have a good understanding of the role color plays in order to make the logo perform its job—giving visual expression to a brand concept.

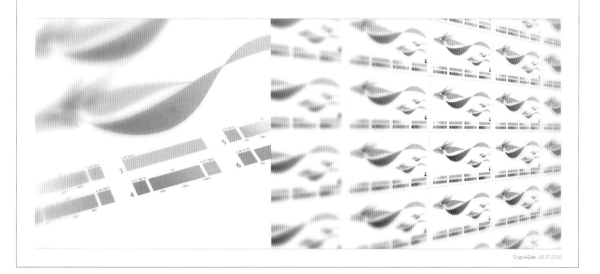

Wordmark Refinement

Color Definition

We are in the process of confirming the exact color percentages for each section of the dragon to ensure accuracy in brightness, value, consistency, saturation and optimal print quality.

Siegel+Gale 08.17.2006

To ensure recognition of the brand, color specifications need to be worked out precisely for all the contexts in which the logo will be reproduced: print, video, plastics, or neon. In many cases, an exact match across all media will be impossible, so the closest approximation must be selected to convey the right overall impression. (See Agility case study on pages 170–173.)

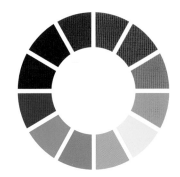

In Western art, painters from the Renaissance to expressionism mastered the use of color to establish moods, direct attention, give an impression of depth or volume, and make creative statements. An understanding of these methods will help any designer produce a more effective logo.

Colors can be classified as warm (reds, oranges, yellows) or cool (blues, greens, violets). Black and white are neutral modifiers, not really considered colors themselves. During the Renaissance, painters began exploring how color perception could be used to give an added sense of depth to a painting. Warmer colors appear to come forward from the picture plane, while cooler colors recede into the background. Objects closer to us in space also appear to have brighter, more saturated colors, while those in the distance are paler and more muted. In designing a multicolor logo, or one rendered with gradations or changes in hue and tone, keeping these rules in mind will help ensure that the desired effect is achieved.

Unfortunately, not every color that appears in nature can be reproduced with inks and dyes in print and plastics, or on a video screen, and colors from any one of these realms—which designers call "color spaces"—aren't necessarily attainable in the others. Luckily, there are several systems that help designers come as close to matching colors as possible: the Pantone Matching System® (PMS) is the most popular. Pantone inks have equivalent specifications for "spot" and "process" printing inks, as well as industrial dyes and computer video, that enable most logo colors to be rendered as faithfully as physically possible in all media.

The important thing to remember is that a visual brand identity works by using color as a device to trigger recognition, tell a story, create a whole impression, and make a decision to participate or buy the product.

As with shapes, colors have both universal meanings and culturally specific associations. Colors have also been shown to have a physiological impact: blues are calming, reds raise our blood pressure, and so on. Specific shades can become strongly associated in our minds with certain experiences; some cultures ascribe mystical powers to certain colors. The juxtaposition of two or more colors in a particular combination often forms the basis for a visual language of color—a palette that can be incorporated into a brand identity to form new meanings, helping ingrain the brand in customers' minds.

Client	Legal Aid Society
Brand story	One of the largest and oldest legal services organizers in New York, serving thousands each year in civil, criminal, and juvenile matters
Studio	Siegel+Gale
Creative director	Doug Sellers
Senior designer	Jong Woo Si
Strategy director	Jenifer Brooks
Typeface	Today Sans
Colors	Multicolored
Design approach	A new identity was intended to give employees something to rally round and to get more positive attention in the media. To help convey the value the Society gives to clients and the broad social change it effects, the designers crafted a bright tapestry of forms that reflect the diversity and complexity of their clientele. The modular system of the logo is easily extended to publication layouts, advertising, and online information design

Diversity

THE LEGAL AID SOCIETY

MAKING THE CASE FOR HUMANITY

Complexity

Assertive

Client	GLAAD (The Gay and Lesbian Alliance Against Defamation)
Brand story	A media advocacy group promoting fair and inclusive portrayals in the media
Studio	Lippincott
Art director	Connie Birdsall
Designers	Jenifer Lehker, Brendán Murphy, and Matt Calkins
Typeface	Futura Extra Bold
Colors	Blue, orange, green, and magenta (process colors)
Design approach	GLAAD needed a simple, clear way to identify the organization as the media arm of the gay, lesbian, and transgender movement. The result expresses how the organization amplifies the voice of the community, playing off a recognized symbol for communication—a megaphone. The logo suggests movement, growth, and momentum, like ripples spreading in a pond, symbolizing the fight for equality and representation. The four versions of the logo represent the diversity, energy, and passion of the community, and give GLAAD the flexibility to speak to a range of topics

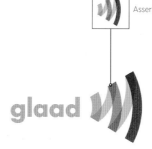

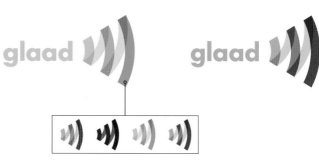

Adaptable

Red

The colors with the shortest wavelength, reds are the most exciting to human eyes and brains. Red is the color of blood, fresh fruit, and the rising sun: it signifies power, passion, and lust for life. Red is an attention-grabber: a red logo will project confidence and dominate its surroundings. Red communicates urgency and for this reason is used by both the Red Cross and the Red Crescent. Red is the color of happiness and prosperity in China and may be used to attract good luck. Red is often the color worn by brides in the East, while it is the color of mourning in South Africa. In Russia, the Bolsheviks used a red flag when they overthrew the Tsar, thus red became associated with Communism. Variations on red include magenta and pink, which are also associated with love, passion, and intimacy.

Orange

Orange is a warm, sunny color, which, being midway between red and yellow, combines many of their associations. It is cheerful, but also calming. Orange is the color of many flowers and foodstuffs. Its meanings tend to be more culturally dependent than those of red: in the USA, orange is associated with Halloween; in Islamic cultures, men die their beards orange to show they have completed the hajj; in Ireland and Ukraine, orange can have political significance. Therefore, using orange as a logo color contains an element of uncertainty if the logo is to be used globally. Variations on orange include amber, beige, and brown (see right), which have their own associated meanings.

Yellow

As a warm color, yellow is also an eye-stopper, and in nature it occurs (together with black) as a warning sign. But culturally its meanings tend to be more ambiguous than those of red or orange. Perhaps counterintuitively, yellow has actually been shown to be a physically calming color. In the writings of Shakespeare (and for many Westerners) yellow is the color of cowardice, whereas in Japan it is associated with courage. Since it resembles gold, yellow is the traditional color of Indian merchants. Yellow presents a problem for designers because it can be difficult to see against a white background: a yellow line must be bordered by a darker color, preferably in a larger area, to have any impact.

Green

The most common color in nature, green is soothing and relaxing. It is often used to denote harmony, balance, tranquility, stability, and, of course, nature itself. Green is a favorite color for indicating natural or organic products. In Islamic cultures, green is seen as a pure color, and therefore symbolizes Islam. Because US banknotes have traditionally used green in their designs, to many, green is "the color of money." Variations of green—avocado, olive, lime, chartreuse—each have their own associations, some of which go in and out of style fairly rapidly. They should be used with care.

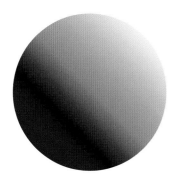

Blue

Probably the most popular logo color, deep blue has the longest wavelengths. Blue is the most profoundly calming color; too much of it can depress spirits, causing "the blues," although in some cultures bright blue is considered a joyful color. In many parts of the world blue denotes authority, dignity, and pride. It is widely associated with intelligence and acknowledged as "corporate" (the nickname of IBM is Big Blue) because of its associations with stability and conservatism. Lighter versions of blue, such as cyan and turquoise, can have magical associations.

Purple

Purple was once a rare color and its highly sought dyes were used for making luxury fabrics. Purple came to be associated with wealth and power, a connotation it still holds today. Mixing blue and red, purple is a passionate color with overtones of sensuality and high emotion. Many purple things in nature are also delicate, such as violets, irises, and other flowers. Lilac and paler variations of purple represent weakness and frailty, so they are not often used in logo designs, unless paired with bolder colors.

Brown

Brown is the admixture of all colors; any pair of opposites on the color wheel (purple and yellow, blue and orange, green and red) will yield brown when mixed together. The color of mud is a surprisingly good color for logos, because it is warmer than black, yet still goes well with all other colors. Besides the obviously earthy associations, which allow it to convey a feeling of visceral authenticity, brown is the color of coffee and chocolate, so it can communicate richness and indulgence. It is also frequently used to denote a proud association with things African.

Black, white, and gray

As noted before, black and white are not really colors, but rather tones that modify other colors. On a functional level, however, they are incorporated as colors in almost every logo, either as an element or as negative space. Gray makes an excellent counterpart to any color, especially a bright one. Being neutral, it has few associations of its own, so it can play a supporting role and allow the other color to grab the glory and tell the story. By adding a subtle hint of another color, grays can be made either warm or cool, which allows them to complement a specific palette even more effectively.

... TYPE

Type has been called the "voice" of text. Typography is the art of selecting and using an appropriate style of type, lettering, or font, in a way that reinforces the intention of the words, enhancing their message through subtleties of feeling conveyed by the specific forms of each letter and by the overall shapes of the words.

Each style of type sends a different message to the reader. Classic, Roman letters have a cultured nuance; simple, modern fonts are clean and direct; calligraphic lettering is romantic, while jagged computer fonts can be funky or technical.

The letterforms of the Latin alphabet carry a lot of historical and cultural baggage that affects their personalities. Serifs (those little fingers and feet adorning the ends of letterforms) date back to Roman times. Blackletter was developed in the Middle Ages based on scribes' handwriting. The modernism of the twentieth century tried either doing away with serifs or greatly exaggerating them, and also developed a multitude of fancy type styles for display at very large sizes: casual, formal, whimsical, geometric. The computer revolution of the 1980s and 1990s brought a further explosion of highly experimental letterforms, all of them with very distinct and memorable personalities, some of them, admittedly, bordering on the illegible.

Other systems, such as Cyrillic and Arabic, seem to have fewer stylistic options, but these options are expanding. Although a novel Latin font may not have a readily available Arabic equivalent in digital form, something comparable for a logo project can usually be custom-crafted by a font designer in a reasonable amount of time. Chinese characters, because of their complexity, offer fewer options for playing with forms, but there has been a surge in the number of available styles since the 1990s.

As the logo designs in the preceding pages make clear, the typographic options available to a logo designer are as varied as the fish in the sea. In the end, choosing the right face for a logo requires being familiar with a great range of typefaces, understanding the personality and feelings imparted by each, and being able to cast the right one in light of the design brief.

Very often, a designer starts with an existing font—either a popular standard or something more unusual from an independent font designer—and then modifies some of the letterforms slightly to make the specific wordmark better integrated, more legible, or more in keeping with the desired character of the brand.

Although it may seem like such modifications are a simple matter, in fact they do require mechanical skill as well as a healthy regard for the subtleties of letterforms, their integrity, and their basis in tradition. But, with a little training and practice, most skilled designers can tackle such alterations.

Besides modifying the letterforms themselves, the spaces between them can be adjusted. Computers are notoriously poor at spacing letters to give an overall effect that is pleasing to the eye. It takes training and practice to be able to see the problems and know how to fix them appropriately.

If the right typographic look cannot be found among the readily available computer fonts, it is always possible to revive an analog font from an earlier era by digitizing it, or commissioning a designer to create a new font from scratch for the logo project.

The important thing is to see letterforms for what they are: complex, finely crafted symbols that convey not just a sound or an idea, but a rich character filled with history and culture.

The history of printed writing is a fascinating story beginning with imitations of handwritten letterforms and developing into the design of modern type styles based on geometric construction, theoretical approaches to legibility, and sheer whimsy. Essentially, Latin, Cyrillic, and Greek typefaces—the scripts used to set English and other European languages—can be sorted into four broad categories: classical serif, modern sans serif, script, or graphically constructed types. Other alphabets (including Arabic, Hebrew, Gujarati, and Thai) and writing systems (such as Chinese, Japanese, and Korean) show a comparable variety of styles, from those based on brush or pen strokes to renderings with a modern, mechanically crafted look.

Serif

Serifs are the little feet and buds protruding from the ends of the lettershapes. Based directly on the stone-carved inscriptions of ancient Rome, with the addition of lowercase letterforms developed in the Middle Ages, these typefaces convey classical elegance, refinement, and erudition. While they are optimal for reading text, many computerized serif fonts are not crafted for display at larger sizes, so they can be less than ideal for logo designs. They may be used as the basis for a customized wordmark if the typographer takes care to manually adjust the spacing between letters, tweak the thick and thin strokes, elide the serifs where they touch, and alter or eliminate other elements as needed to make the whole word look as cohesive and attractive as possible.

Sans serif

The result of early twentieth-century modernism, these fonts generally have an appearance that is cleaner and bolder—more modern—than their serif cousins. They impart a contemporary, international, enlightened feel, although they can also seem a little sterile in comparison with serif typefaces. At large display sizes, sans-serif fonts are usually considered more legible than serif fonts, although this may be a culturally determined matter, rather than any inherent quality of the letterforms.

Script

Whether elegantly calligraphic or casually scrawled, script typefaces reproduce, or at least suggest, handwriting. This is down to the connectors and ligatures tying individual letters together. Script fonts convey a highly personal character, as well as rapidity and convenience. While they can be beautiful, script fonts should be used discerningly in logo designs, since the legibility of particular script styles can be very culturally dependent.

Graphically constructed

Decorative display styles, whether hand-drawn or mechanically constructed, have been a favorite of graphic designers since the dawn of the Industrial Age. Typefaces based purely on geometric forms or fanciful shapes give preference to the creative idea over the rigid discipline of classic letterforms. While legibility may suffer somewhat as a result, the distinct character of such types makes for unique and memorable logo designs, whose stylistic strengths easily outweigh other considerations.

ABCDEFGHIJKLMN
opqrstuvwxyz 1234567

50pt Adobe Garamond Regular: serif

ABCDEFGHIJKLMN
opqrstuvwxyz 12345

50pt Berthold Akzidenz Grotesk Regular: sans serif

ABCDEFGHIJKLMN
opqrstuvwxyz 1234567890

50pt Metroscript: script

ABCDEFGHIJKLMN
opqrstuvwxyz 123

50pt Eviltype Light: graphically constructed

... ALTERNATE FORMATS

As we've already seen, the majority of logos consist of an icon and a name (perhaps with an endorsement, translation, or sub-brand), placed together in some convenient and visually pleasing way. Sometimes the two elements are interlocked in such a way that there is really only one simple, obvious way to arrange them; but more often there will be a couple of possibilities, and designers will want to consider more than one of them in determining how to present the logo optimally in different contexts.

These layouts are sometimes called lockups, an old-fashioned printers' term implying that once the right arrangement is determined, it should remain locked up and not be fussed with, especially by nondesigners. It is quite acceptable for a logo to have different layouts to be used in different contexts, as long as there is some logic and consistency to this, and the customer is not left confused.

The context in which a logo will appear is important in determining the best arrangement for the symbol and wordmark. On a typical letterhead, a compact logo in a rectangular format usually works nicely. Over a doorway, on a banner, in a stadium, or on a website, a horizontal strip will maximize the size of the lettering. In some types of signage, a very tall, narrow arrangement may be called for. Determining in which contexts the logo will be displayed is an essential early part of the logo design process.

Audiences in different countries also have varying degrees of sophistication in regard to visual branding. People who live in media-saturated markets are more accustomed to absorbing brand identities rapidly, and will quickly recognize a logo in which the symbol dominates or even stands alone. In areas where there is less familiarity with branding, it may be necessary to emphasize the name and make the symbol secondary. The three signage options for Agility are a good example of this.

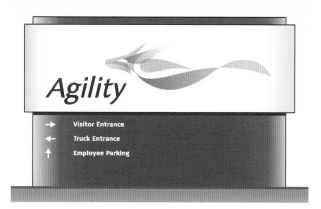

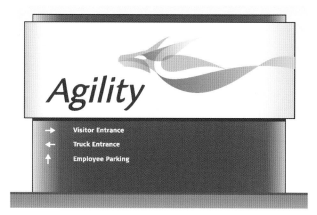

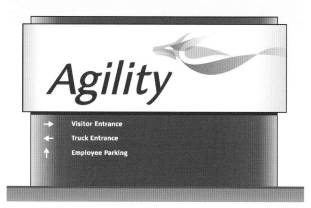

Three options for using the Agility logo on building signage are distinguished by subtle differences in proportion between the wordmark and the dragon symbol. The choice of which to use in a particular market depends on the local brand manager's judgment about how prominent the name need be in comparison with the symbol. (See Agility case study on pages 170–173.)

... DEVELOPING A FULL IDENTITY

For more than a century, ever since the German industrial firm AEG adopted the world's first corporate identity, designers have been patiently explaining to clients that a logo cannot perform effectively in isolation. It needs to be part of a complete visual identity program, whose elements can include:

- typography for posters, brochures, and letterheads
- a palette of supplemental colors
- a system of auxiliary motifs and markings
- product design and packaging
- photographic or illustrative styles
- advertising layouts
- interface design for websites and mobile applications
- signs and wayfinding systems
- store interiors and exhibition environments
- slide presentations
- vehicle liveries
- uniforms
- ... even auditory and olfactory elements

In short, a visual identity includes all the things that extend the brand identity into its full range of contexts. These are places where the logo alone cannot go, would present the brand inadequately, or would suffer from overuse, breeding contempt rather than providing positive reinforcement.

The supporting elements of the brand identity are most effective when they clearly complement the logo, either with a direct visual clue or by being designed and executed in a similar style. Over time, as viewers grow accustomed to associating the secondary aspects of the identity with the brand, it becomes possible to use the logo more and more sparingly, saving it from becoming too tiresome.

It is usually impossible to prepare all elements of a complex identity at once. The needs of a brand constantly change, and all the contexts in which the brand will be present and visible to customers—"touchpoints" in the jargon of the branding business—won't be known at the outset. As the designer becomes immersed in learning about and building the brand, there should be ample opportunities for revision and addition. Medium and large clients are often best served by keeping a designer or branding agency on retainer.

Printed brand manuals that specify all the elements of a brand identity are nice ways of presenting the designer's work, but they usually end up gathering dust after a brief period of use. Far more practical and effective are online references, which can be quickly and inexpensively updated.

Rich heritage

Client	Fraser Yachts
Brand story	A provider of luxury yacht services around the world
Studio	Inaria
Creative directors	Andrew Thomas, Debora Berardi, and Andy Bain
Designers	Andy Bain and Pablo Basla
Typeface	Gill Sans (modified)
Colors	Deep blue (PMS 296), cerise (PMS Rubine Red), silver (PMS 877), and gray (PMS Cool Gray 11)
Design approach	Since the designers who created the logo and brand identity will not always be the same ones who produce every item of brand communication in the future, the brand manual lays out the specific rules for using the logo as well as all the secondary elements of the identity, such as the typography, colors, photographic style, wave pattern and bands used as secondary graphics, ad layouts, and designs for brochures and PowerPoint slides. These supplemental elements carry the look of the brand beyond areas where the logo can work alone. They all work with the logo to promote the brand values (desirable, knowledgeable, innovative) and brand personality (stylish, authoritative, creative-thinking). Using these elements as carefully and consistently as the logo itself ensures that the visual presentation of the brand always has the optimum impact and effectiveness across all brand touchpoints

Innovative

... CHARACTERS & MOTIFS

Sometimes a logo needs a friend. Perhaps the brand personality needs to be recast as more approachable or more intimate, or the brand just wants to put on a friendlier face. Changing the logo can be difficult and expensive—and unnecessary. A better solution can be to give the brand a mascot.

A new character can spark fresh interest in the brand, reinvigorating it in the eyes of customers. It can be an animated variation of the logo, or an entirely different character. Although not all mascots are childlike, they appeal to the inner child with a sense of familiarity, fun, and play.

Mascots tend to be cartoon-like and can walk a fine line between being appealing and being ridiculous. In many cases, a mascot serves for a limited time as the basis of a campaign or a seasonal sales promotion.

On the other hand, a successful mascot can assume a dominant role in representing the brand and be adopted permanently. Ronald McDonald, the famous clown who embodied the McDonald's fast-food brand in TV commercials for decades, is also the namesake of the company's charity foundation and its residences for the families of children with cancer.

Playful

Friendly

Client	Flash Dab Games & Entertainment
Brand story	A digital agency that develops social games
Studio	InsaneFacilities
Designer	Jarek Berecki
Typeface	Bespoke, based on Bello Pro
Color	Black
Design approach	The company has a fun, casual approach typical of many young firms in the field of game programming. To capture this the designer, who is based in Poland, turned to cartoons and exotic animals for inspiration. The result is an engaging mascot that invites further exploration

Supplementing the logo with a secondary device or graphic motif has many benefits. The additional motif can extend the brand to places where the logo can't go, or wouldn't perform adequately. Stripes, swashes, and waves are a typical part of many brand identities, but a supplemental motif can be much more than that. Depending on the brand personality and character, a motif can be a highly decorative organic or floral form, a technical or mechanical device, or a human element such as a hand or face.

Innovation

Client Godrej

Brand story An Indian conglomerate producing everything from hair color to refrigerators, whose 400 million customers include farmers and hipsters, housewives and software engineers

Studio Interbrand

Designers Andy Howell and Edward Bolton

Typeface Hand-drawn script

Colors Crimson, green, and blue

Design approach The Godrej brand, whose heritage reaches back more than a century, covers an extremely diverse range of products, so its values are based on essential qualities that transcend any single sector or category: trust, integrity, and humility. To express the ambition and innovation that drive the company forward, the logo—an unassuming signature—is complemented by a repertory of shapes and figures that dance and dazzle, capturing a sense of worldliness while retaining a very Indian look and feel

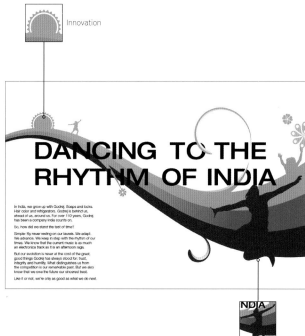

DANCING TO THE RHYTHM OF INDIA

In India, we grow up with Godrej. Soaps and locks. Hair color and refrigerators. Godrej is behind us, ahead of us, around us. For over 110 years, Godrej has been a company India counts on.

So, how did we stand the test of time?

Simple: By never resting on our laurels. We adapt. We advance. We keep in step with the rhythm of our times. We know that the current music is as much an electronica track as it is an afternoon raga.

But our evolution is never at the cost of the great, good things Godrej has always stood for: trust, integrity, and humility. What distinguishes us from the competition is our remarkable past. But we also know that we owe the future our sincerest best.

Like it or not, we're only as good as what we do next.

Exuberance

... MIXED MEDIA & 3D

Since the 1990s, thanks to developments in the technology of reproducing images and the ease of giving an object a 3D look on a computer or mobile screen, logos with 3D styling have become ubiquitous. Whether the 3D look turns out to be a passing stylistic fad remains to be seen; for the moment at least, it can be found on everything from automobile badges to nonprofit logos.

Beyond the popularity of the "button" style, designers can also achieve compelling images of a logo by building it either as a virtual 3D rendering, or out of physical objects. These objects can then be photographed from various angles and with a variety of special effects of lighting and focus to give a brand identity an abstract, but visually fascinating set of illustrations.

Building a logo out of blocks is just the beginning. Neon lights are a favorite medium for logos because of their brightness and visibility, even in daylight. Neon has its limitations: forms must be reduced to curved lines and sharp angles, with all gradations eliminated, and the palette of effective colors is limited: deep colors like navy blue or brown are physically impossible.

Animation of the logo was once restricted to the final seconds of television advertisements, but since the advent of the web, incorporating motion into a logo has become more popular. Whether a simple sparkle or a lengthy routine, animations add a measure of novelty.

Client	Honest Advice, Honest Aid, Honest Assessment
Brand story	Three sister companies offering different services, but sharing the same initials. Honest Aid is a US-registered nonprofit company that began in Zanzibar, assessing local community needs; Honest Advice provides advisory services via the Internet; Honest Assessment is a for-profit consultancy that reviews and recommends improvements to NGO projects
Studio	Raidy Printing Group
Art director	MarieJoe Raidy
Designers	Eric Pochez and Ziad Richmany
Typeface	Futura
Colors	Blue, red, and green (process blends)
Design approach	All three companies provide their services in a user-friendly, web-based manner, with animated digital avatars interacting with customers. The bubble-style logos convey a fun experience and give an impression of trustworthiness. The concept—color and a complementary icon—could be economically adapted to further services in the future

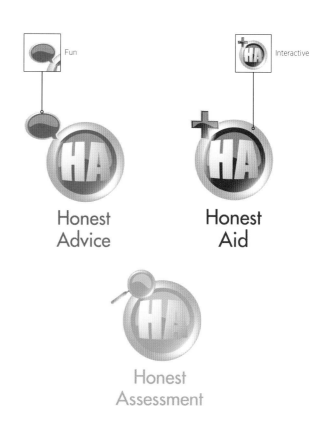

Honest
Advice

Honest
Aid

Honest
Assessment

Client	Croatian Institute for Construction
Brand story	The Institut Gradjevinarstva Hrvatske (IGH) provides services in planning, supervision, and support for the construction of roads, bridges, buildings, and other civil engineering projects
Studio	Studio International
Designer	Boris Ljubicic
Typeface	Futura Md BT
Colors	Red (PMS 485), blue (PMS 287), and gray (PMS Cool Gray 9)
Design approach	The logo design captures both the occupation of the Institute and its national origin, subtly incorporating the visual code of the coat of arms of Croatia. To further illustrate what the organization does, the geometric shapes have been reconstructed several times using blocks, glass prisms, and metallic tubes, producing a series of photographic images that capture the intelligence and inquisitiveness of the brand while being abstract enough to serve in a variety of contexts (such as posters, brochures, and reports) where the basic logo would not provide sufficient visual interest on its own

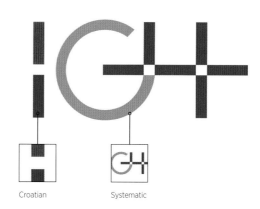

Croatian

Systematic

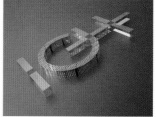

Neon has a persistent charm and a strong
association with nightlife that is highly
appropriate for certain types of brands.

Client	Troika Dialog
Brand story	The oldest and largest private investment bank in Russia
Studio	Interbrand
Art director	Christoph Marti
Designers	Iris Burkard, Michaela Burger, Alexander Kohl, Dimitar Tsvetkov, and Marco Zimmerli
Typeface	Daxline
Colors	Silver (PMS 877), red (PMS 185), green (PMS 354), and process blue
Design approach	The interconnection promised by the brand and the triangular structures suggested by the name are exploited for maximum effect in this animated version of the logo. The endlessly varied solutions of the company's services are given dynamic, exciting form, and the resulting video clip can be used in presentations, on the web, and in videos and DVDs promoting the company

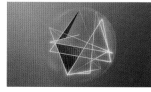

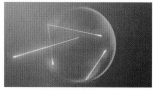
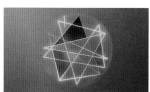

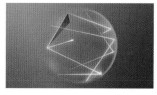

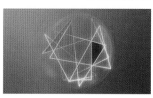

... TAGLINES

Beyond what can be clearly communicated by the icon and the name, companies often want to augment their logo with a few words that reinforce the brand values, exhort the public, categorize the product, give out the web address, or otherwise make a statement about what the logo stands for. This is most commonly seen in advertising and packaging, but a brief verbal addendum can accompany the logo in almost any context.

This added verbiage can go by many names: claim, motto, tagline, strapline, signoff ... Regardless of what it's called, there are some things to keep in mind to ensure that it augments, rather than detracts from the logo.

Some designers try to incorporate the claim directly into the logo design, but this is almost always a liability visually, and invariably causes problems at small sizes or outside the most benign contexts. Instead, it is best to keep the logo to just a name and/or icon, and work out one or more variant formats in which the claim is added harmoniously, at a modest distance from the logo. These "lockups" of logo and tagline are then included in the guidelines for the overall brand identity.

Luxurious

Client	Coogan & Morrow
Brand story	"Stunning flowers for sensational events" tells the whole story of what this English company does
Agency	Jan Barker & David Caunce
Art director	Jan Barker
Designer	David Caunce
Typefaces	Mrs Eaves, Palatino (ampersand), and Goudy Sans (tagline)
Colors	Black and pink (custom process color)
Design approach	Drawing inspiration from natural flower forms, the logo for this new company incorporates ornamental decoration, simple typography, and a claim. The claim explains what the company does and also presents the brand position, making a promise and feeding the aspirations of their customers. Since the logo is applied in a limited range of contexts—website, letterhead, cards, brochures, and signs—the designers don't have to worry about it working at very small sizes, at low resolution, or in such media as neon

stunning flowers for sensational events   Classical

... REFRESHING A LOGO

The best logos in the world inevitably decay over time, victims of neglect or simple entropy. Why? Because in good times and bad, our minds and our ways of seeing are perpetually moving forward. Our tastes and expectations are constantly developing, incessantly stimulated and informed by the rapidly changing world around us. Even without a brand crisis, a logo that doesn't change is actually drifting slowly backward in time, and will eventually appear tired and outdated.

There's no magic formula for determining how fast this will occur, or to what degree. It is up to experienced designers and brand managers, with a practiced eye for current styles and a good sense of a brand's essence and personality, to determine when the time is ripe for an update.

What's old can readily become new again. Seldom is it necessary to toss out an old logo and start over from scratch. Often, subtle changes—unnoticed by all but the savviest observers—are all that's needed to keep a logo moving forward.

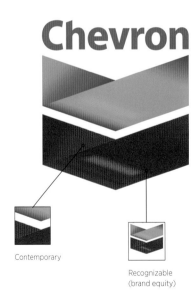

Contemporary

Recognizable
(brand equity)

Client	Chevron
Brand story	After a merger between Chevron and Texaco, company management wanted to present a unified face to the world, with a more contemporary image that would retain existing brand equity, but focus on the future
Studio	Lippincott
Art directors	Alex de Jánosi and Connie Birdsall
Designers	Alex de Jánosi, Adam Stringer, Lisa Lind, Kevin Hammond, and Jenifer Lehker
Strategy	Kim Rendleman
Typeface	Myriad (redrawn)
Colors	Blue (PMS 2935), red (PMS 186), deep red (PMS 202), and cyan (process color)
Design approach	Giving the existing chevron mark shading and dimension makes it at once more aligned with customers' expectations of a modern brand, yet maintains recognition of the icon from a distance that loyal motorists rely on. The new mark is warmer and more approachable, embodying the idea of "human energy." The refreshed logo is further supported by a comprehensive new identity and an online brand center to aid in implementation at all touchpoints

Refreshing an existing identity, retaining enough of its equity to keep it familiar, but altering or adding elements to keep it current, involves the same process as creating a new one: analyze the brand performance, articulate its essence and personality, characterize its customers, determine which elements communicate the desired qualities to them, decide what to add and what to take away, and redraw the logo so that all is well again.

Then wait a while. And repeat.

Client	Delta
Brand story	After emerging from bankruptcy and restructuring, Delta was in need of strategic repositioning and a redesign of its image and customer experience
Studio	Lippincott
Art directors	Connie Birdsall, Adam Stringer, and Fabian Diaz
Designers	Adam Stringer, Fabian Diaz, Kevin Hammond, Michael Milligan, and Michael Tharp
Production	Brendan deVallance and Jeremy Darty
Typeface	Whitney (redrawn)
Colors	Deep red (PMS 202), red (PMS 186), and deep blue (PMS 654)
Design approach	The new logo was designed to convey renewed strength, confidence, and the modernization of the airline, both to customers and to its own employees. The simplified all-red symbol and uppercase wordmark visually reinforce a more sophisticated, purposeful, and globally appropriate brand expression, while remaining recognizable and considerate of the airline's 70-year heritage. The symbol of the delta is angled and artfully cropped in advertising and airplane livery to emphasize momentum and suggest growth and optimism

Modern

International

DIRECTORY OF CONTRIBUTORS

Mid-to-large and global firms

Fitch [www.fitch.com]
360°, Ali Bin Ali, Asyad, Deek Duke, KMC, al Muhaidib, Northgate, Qatar Symphony, Qipco, QTA

Inaria [www.inaria.co.uk]
Flowers of the World, Fraser Yachts, Mason Rose, One&Only Cape Town, Vanquish, WildCRU

Interbrand [www.interbrand.com]
China Merchants Securities, Cresta Hotels, Daiwa House Group, Geeknet, Godrej, Hays, Huawei, Idea, Implenia, Neva Killa Dream, Nigerian Airlines, Schindler, Seattle Childrens, Sochi 2014, This is Rugby, Troika

Landor Associates [www.landor.com]
City of Melbourne, Miller & Green, One Degree, Worldeka

Lippincott [www.lippincott.com]
Bank of New York, Bayn, BrightHeart, Chartis, Chevron, Delta, First Citizens, GLAAD, Hayneedle, Johnson Controls, Mashreq, Power, QuickChek, TACA, UMW, Vale, Walmart, Wana, Xohm

Minale Tattersfield [www.mintat.co.uk]
Artoil, Harlequins Rugby, Luisa, Luxair, Oz, Santa Margherita, Torresella, Sassoregale, Trentino

Siegel+Gale [www.siegelgale.com]
Agility, ITFC, Kaust, Legal Aid Society, Neustar, Pfizer, Phoenix House, Port of Long Beach, Rave, Turn Around

TippingSprung [www.tippingsprung.com]
Arctaris, Brastilo

Small to mid-size firms and individuals

Aeraki (Despina Aeraki), Athens, Greece [www.aeraki.gr]
Anninos Hairchitecture

Ambient (Scott Mosher), NY, New York, USA
[www.scottmosher.com]
Rock Zone

William Anderson, New Hampshire, USA
[www.andersoncreative.com]
Fragile X Foundation, Lobkowitz Beer

Artiva Design (Daniele De Batté, Davide Sossi), Genova, Italy
[www.artiva.it]
Energy\Company, King-Dome, TonMöbel

//Avec (Camillia BenBassat), New York, USA [www.avec.us]
Chocosho, Cooper Square Hotel, Elemental, Studio 5 in 1, Studio Ma

Jan Barker and David Caunce, Manchester, UK
[www.imagine-cga.co.uk]
Coogan & Morrow

Erik Borreson, Wisconsin, USA [www.erikborreson.com]
Central Wisconsin State Fair, Erik Borreson Design

Bulletpoint Design (Paul Kerfoot), Bradford, UK
[www.bullet-man.com]
Odsal Sports Village

Church Logo Gallery (Michael Kern), California, USA
[www.churchlogogallery.com]
Bethel Assembly of God, Explore Children's Ministry

Creative Squall (Tad Dobbs), Texas, USA [www.creativesquall.com]
Creative Squall, Joe Allison and This Machine

Colin Decker, Texas, USA [www.frankandproper.com]
Gaslamp Computers, Team Dank

Designation (Mike Quon), New Jersey, USA [www.quondesign.com]
Settlement Housing Fund

Alexander Egger, Vienna, Austria
[www.satellitesmistakenforstars.com]
Acherer, Arm the Lonely, Das Comptoir, Evolve, Impulse, Nussberger, Pilot Projekt, Puhm, Re:cycle, redhot

Nils-Petter Ekwall, Malmö, Sweden [www.nilspetter.se]
Falco Invernale, Ich Robot, TRON

Executive Strategy (Ng Lung-Wai), Hong Kong, China
[www.esl.ecob.com.hk]
Hong Kong Wetland Park

Jeff Fisher LogoMotives, Oregon, USA
[www.jfisherlogomotives.com]
Balaboosta Delicatessen, VanderVeer Center

Fivefootsix (Algy Batten), London, UK [www.fivefootsix.co.uk]
Banana Split Productions, GotSpot, Graham Gill Carpets, Project Compass

Andy Gabbert, California, USA [www.andygabbertdesign.com]
Business Continuity Management, Center for Teaching Excellence, Chef
Tested, Family Art Affair, Kool Kat Jackson, Lunch & Lecture

Carol García del Busto, Barcelona, Spain [—]
RedAIEP, Siece

Virginia Green, Texas, USA [www.vgreendesign.com]
Black Hare Studio, Grace Community Church, Haynie Drilling Co.

Mary Hutchison Design, Washington, USA
[www.maryhutchisondesign.com]
Katherine Anderson Landscape Architecture, Bad Breed, Bristlecone
Advisors, IBC, Large Left Brain, O'Asian Kitchen, Røen Associates,
The Valley Club

idApostle (Steve Zelle), Ottawa, Canada [www.idapostle.com]
idApostle, Westboro Nursery School

Imagine-cga (David Caunce), Manchester, UK
[www.imagine-cga.co.uk]
Forever Manchester, Makin Architecture, Okotie's, Seven Star Soccer,
Barry White

InsaneFacilities (Jarek Berecki), Łódź, Poland
[www.insanefacilities.com]
FlashDab, Imminent, Neuroad, Technique, Vivio

Irving & Co. (Julian Roberts), London, UK [www.irving.co.uk]
Artisan Biscuits, Byron Proper Hamburgers, Duchy Originals, Fiona Cairns,
No. Twelve Queen Street

Juno Studio (Jun Li), New Jersey, USA [www.junostudio.com]
Development Partner Program, IntelliVue Unplugged

Kanella (Kanella Arapoglou), Athens, Greece [www.kanella.com]
The Olive Family

Tadas Karpavicius, Kaunas, Lithuania [www.t-karpavicius.com]
Klaipeda Goes Indie, Oro Pagalves, Promo Phobia

Brett King, Christchurch, NZ [www.frankandproper.com]
Hayden King, One Amigo, Retreasured

Kniven (Emilia Lundgren and Karolina Wahlberg Westenhoff),
Mölndal, Sweden [www.kniven.se, www.karolinaw.se]
Uppvunnet

Korolivski Mitci (Viktoriia Korol, Dmytro Korol), Kiev, Ukraine
[www.mitci.com.ua]
Eurofeed, Gala Realty, Green Town, Korolivski Mitci, Pivduima,
Quantum Solar, Smartmatic, Tasman

Lavmi Creative Zone (Babeta Ondrová and Jan Slovák), Prague,
Czech Republic [www.lavmi.com]
Czech Basketball Federation, Czech Ministry of the Interior, CzechPoint,
Dock, NERV, ProTrip

McBreen Design (Craig McBreen), Washington, USA
[www.mcbreendesign.com]
Environmental Construction

Clay McIntosh Creative, Oklahoma, USA [www.claymcintosh.com]
Lies That Rhyme, Risk Management Planning

Renaud Merle, Robion, France [www.renaudmerle.fr]
Accompagnement Individualisé à Domicile (AID), Renaud Merle

MINE (Christopher Simmons and Tim Belonax), California, USA
[www.minesf.com]
California Film Institute, C+ Jewelry, Center for Cognitive Computing, Fino,
Go Green, Humanity+, Kink, Mill Valley Film Festival, Open Square, Rafael
Film Center, San Francisco Parks Trust, Year

Mosaic Creative (Tad Dobbs), Texas, USA [www.creativesquall.com]
CashPlus, Gretta Sloane, H+M Racing, Nobles & Baldwin

Tom Munckton, London, UK [www.tommunckton.co.uk]
Stories: Projects in Film

Mariam bin Natoof, Dubai, UAE [www.natoof.com]
La Bouchee, Natoof Design, Zilar

Obos Creative (Ethem Hürsü Öke), Istanbul, Turkey
[www.oboscreative.com]
Akadental, VNL Telecom

Paragon Marketing Communications, Salmiya, Kuwait [www.paragonmc.com]
Amwaj, Anubis Blog, Atyab Investments, Better Homes, Fresh Productions, La Baguette, Rumors

Pencil (Luke Manning), Bath, UK [www.penciluk.co.uk]
Keco, Rock & Road, Ray Watkins

PenguinCube, Beirut, Lebanon [www.penguincube.com]
Dekkaneh, IPSIS, Telephone.com

Planet (Phil Bradwick), Hungerford, UK [www.planet-ia.com]
St. George's Academy, Mark Snow, Velda Lauder Corsetieres

Playout (Tiago Machado), Maia, Portugal [www.playout.pt]
EmFesta, Rui Grazina—Arquitectura+Design

R Design, London, UK [www.r-design.co.uk]
BHS Kids, Cocoa Deli, Designers at Debenhams, Kelly Hoppen Home, Little Me, Micheline Arcier Aromathérapie, Spa Formula, Sweet Millie

Marc Rabinowitz, New York, UK [www.ijustmight.com]
Chabad at the University of Miami

Raidy Printing Group (MarieJoe Raidy), Beirut, Lebanon [www.raidy.com]
Honest Advice, Honest Aid, Honest Assessment

Riverbed Design (Corbet Curfman), Washington, USA [www.riverbeddesign.com]
Community Skate & Snow, Northwest Hub

Seven25. Design & Typography (Isabelle Swiderski), Vancouver, Canada [www.seven25.com]
Cherie Smith Jewish Book Fair, Fair Trade Jewellery, Garbage Critic, Home for the Games, LOUD Foundation, TennisXL, Vancouver Foundation

Leila Singleton, California, USA [www.leilasingleton.com]
Wink

Starr Tincup (Tad Dobbs), Texas, USA [www.creativesquall.com]
Kilowatt Bikes, Starr Tincup

Stebler Creative (Jeremy Stebler) [—]
Hotelicopter

Studio EMMI (Emmi Salonen), London, UK [www.emmi.co.uk]
Agile Films, Concrete Hermit, Lankabaari, Matteria

Studio International, Zagreb, Croatia [www.studio-international.com]
Croatian National Tourist Board, IGH, Town of Kutina, Museum Documentation Center, Optima Telecom, Šimecki

Studio Punkat (Hugo Roussel), Nancy, France [www.punkat.com]
Association de Musique Ancienne de Nancy

The House (Steven Fuller and Sam Dyer), Bath, UK [www.thehouse.co.uk]
Calbarrie, Julian House, Paladin Group, The Prince's Youth Business, The Best Of

Think Studio (John Clifford), New York, USA [www.thinkstudionyc.com]
Alex Coletti Productions, Erickson Longboards, Mariam Haskell, Porcupine Group, The Retro, Soulpicnic

Transfer Studio (Valeria Hedman, Falko Grentrup), London, UK [www.transferstudio.co.uk]
The Smalls, Tapio, Transfer Studio

Chris Trivizas Design, Athens, Greece [www.christrivizas.gr]
220, FilmCenter, Housale, Oniro The Bar, Vrionis Music House

Wibye Advertising & Graphic Design, London, UK [www.wibyeadvertising.com]
Green Gas

Nancy Wu Design, Vancouver, Canada [www.nancywudesign.com]
North Shore Spirit Trail, Paul Wu + Associates, Tenth Church

INDEX